THE
ISLAND
HOUSE

THE
ISLAND
HOUSE

Our wild new life
on a tiny Cornish isle

MARY CONSIDINE

monoray

First published in Great Britain in 2022
by Monoray, an imprint of
Octopus Publishing Group Ltd
Carmelite House
50 Victoria Embankment
London EC4Y 0DZ
www.octopusbooks.co.uk

An Hachette UK Company
www.hachette.co.uk

ISBN 978-1-80096-014-5

A CIP catalogue record for this book is available from the British Library.

Printed and bound in the UK

10 9 8 7 6 5 4 3 2 1

Typeset in 10.75/16.5pt Miller Text by Jouve (UK), Milton Keynes

This FSC® label means that materials used for
the product have been responsibly sourced.

This **monoray** book was crafted and published by Jake Lingwood,
Alex Stetter, Jane Selley, Caroline Taggart, Jonathan Christie,
Stephen Millership, Helen Cann, Two Associates, and Lisa Pinnell.

For Patrick

Contents

ST GEORGE'S ISLAND

LANDING
BEACH

Chapel
Site

HIGH
COVE

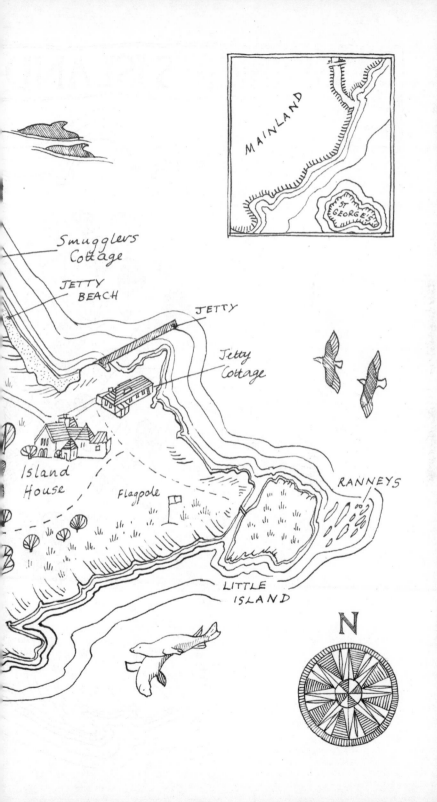

Chapter 1

Getting There

———

The side-view's like the island's profile
as the boat approaches: that long beak
stretching south to the Rannies and behind it
the abrupt hill with its sycamore wood.

Chris Considine, *The Skull*

In the January dark, a young man walks slowly into the sea. Navigating by receding street lights, he can just make out the surface of the slope down to the shingle from the road at Hannafore, and then the rough path over the first rocks, but the water itself is unlit. He listens to the heavy sound of his boots through the waves, stumbling to an ungainly fall forwards, noisy splashing, a boot slipping from his foot. As the other fills, he kicks it away, and is swimming, his breath hurting from the cold.

He can't see where he is going, but he knows the island is calling.

In the hour before dawn, he closes his eyes, and follows the birds. He thinks he might have been swimming for days, in his waterlogged jumper. He knows he is in the right place, that he has done the right thing, following the signals that pointed him to this journey; but perhaps it has no end, only the impersonal suck of the water, and his legs too tired to take him much further. He floats, and touches rock.

Pilgrims took the same route once, perched in perilous boats or wading across a sea floor which was higher, centuries ago, than now. How many monks reached the tiny island chapel where they were sent to worship; how many added their bones to the litter of unmourned graves under the springy grass? Did the little wind-blown cell call to them, or were their eyes fixed from the start on their return journey to the safety of the mainland at Hannafore, the 'haven afore'? Did they feel the same certainty that Ross does that the island was the place they needed to be, or were they just doing as they were told?

The first building he comes to houses a generator, but his brain is too cold to understand it. The next is an empty cottage, with promisingly soft bin bags. He knows he has come to the right place, that he is expected, when he finds a pair of trousers and a thick, torn sheet.

In the early winter light, our yellow dog gives a cursory bark as he finishes his breakfast.

'There's nothing there, Skippy!' Patrick tells him, as we tell him several times a day in the lonely winters when he hears a sinister sound outside: a wheelbarrow moving in the wind, a cat scratching the doormat. We are alone here on the island from October to January, and Skipp is hyper-alert, knowing he needs to protect us.

'Look!' Patrick opens the front door to demonstrate – and a large young man with dreadlocks and a matted beard, dressed in a pink sheet and grass-green trousers a foot too short, holds out his hand.

'Hallo, I'm Ross. Could I possibly have a cup of tea?'

He shouldn't have survived: January, high tide, full night. The island looks so close to Hannafore, the coastal road from the town which runs out to the west. A few times a year, at the irregular extreme spring tides, you can walk across, and in their time, the ladies of the island handed out daffodils to the traditional Easter walkers. In perfect conditions, if you keep to the perfect route, you barely get your feet wet; if there is a little more movement in the water, or height to the tide, you might find yourself waist deep. Coming to the island on an official boat, you come the long way round: down the river first, then out of the harbour mouth, the rocks of West Looe to starboard and the beach at East Looe to port, before you cross the open sea: an indirect mile from shore to shore. But the land directly opposite the north face of the island appears to be no distance away.

At a full high tide, which might be six metres above the base level, it's a challenging swim even in summer daylight, undertaken perhaps by a group of swimmers for charity, or an

Ironman with a point to prove. In winter, in the dark, it ought to be a death warrant.

We sit Ross in front of the gas fire, wrapped first in a blanket and then in the warmest thermals and jumpers we can find, with a hot-water bottle, a cup of tea and a delighted Labrador. We can't stop him talking, about the hints and coincidences, the suggestions and alignments, which convinced him he must come to the island. His family live not far away, you can see the island from their house, and he has begun to feel a spiritual pull, a magical power, from this tiny, lonely place. Again and again, he tells us, over the past weeks he's heard or seen allusions to islands, to ruined chapels, to families who once lived here. He had to come.

Ross, poised in his twenties between the pull of his childhood home and the unknown world, is seeking sanctuary, and we are oddly unsurprised to see him. I would like him to stay for long enough to explore the island, to see if he can find what he came looking for, but Patrick is more practical. Aside from questions of Ross's safety, his need perhaps for help beyond a cup of tea, we know from past experience that there's a good chance that someone will have seen him as the sun came up, from one of the many houses which overlook the bay, and reported the body in the water; that the lifeboat will be out in the bay looking for a suicide.

Common sense dictates that we contact Dave, the lifeboat coxswain, straight away, and although Ross doesn't want to cause trouble, insists that an uncle could collect him, Dave tells us firmly, 'We'll come right out,' and Ross's island trip is over.

We pack him off on to the lifeboat, where he seems suddenly fragile in a life jacket, and the attendant paramedic diagnoses hypothermia and dispatches him straight to hospital.

Attie, the last owner of the house and fifteen years dead when Ross arrives on the doorstep, would have been thrilled by his pilgrimage. The Atkins sisters owned the island for forty years, coming to Cornwall from Surrey, middle-aged, unmarried. Attie, just retired, believed passionately that the island had the power to draw people to it; that she and her sister Babs, for instance, were *meant* to buy it. It could also, she insisted, reject you: occasionally a day visitor arrives on the island but cannot bring themselves to advance beyond the landing beach, huddling there until a boat can take them back to the world. Attie was convinced that the place could inspire, heal, give those who came to it the thing they were looking for. Terrifying, irresistible even in her eighties, she would have glowed at Ross, bewitched him; she would not have rung the coastguard. She would also have had no doubt that he would come back, be compelled to come back, but we aren't sure whether we will ever see Patrick's second-best jumper again.

Twenty-two acres, a mile round, the island could just be a large field, were it not for the steep hill at the west, the darkness of the woodland to the north, the distinct areas of grassland and shingle, gardens and cliffs, beaches and buildings – and the wide moat of sea. Because of that, that isolation, it is automatically romantic, fat with legend and history: the child Christ playing on the beach; the ley lines which meet at the standing stone above it; the ancient chapel now buried under the hill, and the centuries of bones beneath; ghosts, and treasure. For the monks who kept the chapel here, for the free traders hiding smuggled brandy beneath the false floors of old barns, for Ross, for the Atkins sisters and for us, it is a tiny world where the wider one barely, sometimes, seems to exist. There is no traffic, no commerce; no mains water, electricity or broadband, and often no other people. Life is dictated by the seasons: drinking water might completely run out in a dry summer; you are only warm in the winter if you bring in wood and stoke the fires continually; if the generator isn't maintained, there is no light when the sun goes down. If you argue with your partner, there is nowhere to escape.

'This is not a place to run away to,' we are warned, just before we move into Island House. 'This is not an easy place.' Patrick's friends stage an intervention at our leaving party from London. 'Don't go,' they tell him. 'It's cold, it's isolated, the internet will be rubbish.' But the island has been my sanctuary all my life, or for as long as I can remember, unchanging, unchangeable, part of myself, and now it has started to talk to Patrick too, of practical solutions to practical problems, but also of the light on the water, the intricacies of wind and tide, the lament of the gulls.

So, by the time Ross arrives, we are entering our fifth year in Island House, set only yards back from low cliffs on either side, with its high Victorian gables and its white sides flashing in the low sun. We have made our home here, only a mile or so from the bucket-and-spade resort of Looe, with its sandy beach and pasty shops, but this is a different world, a different time.

The way to the island boat – if you have planned and booked your crossing, if you are driving respectably down to your family summer holiday – winds through Looe's narrow streets. These were never designed for cars and have been triumphantly reclaimed by the slow feet of tourists, scarlet from the sun. You squeeze between shops selling Cornish fudge and ice cream, little changed over fifty years or more, into shrinking widths of tarmac, sweating your slow way at walking pace with a car full of children, tins of oxtail soup, bags of powdered milk. At last, fraught with the pressures of kamikaze tourists, car-sick passengers and the retreating tide, you find yourself driving straight towards the river. When you stop with the car peering over the edge, you see a throng of boats and think, panicking: 'Which one?'

The experience advertised in the *Farm Holiday Guide* of 1979 sounded idyllic, irresistible: 'Privately owned island with natural rock swimming pool'. There were only three houses there, my mother learned from the guidebook, and two beaches; no roads, no shops, the most primitive sanitation, but palm trees and sea thrift, oystercatchers, sandpipers and seals. It would be worth the effort of bullying my father into going away for what she must have suspected might be our last holiday together as a family; worth the car-sickness and long, hot hours of his nervous driving, to come to this isolation, this peace. My grandparents had warned her about marrying my father, a brilliant, penniless academic with a restless Irish yearning for something he never found, something that might satisfy some insatiable hunger: religion, perhaps; scholarship; romantic love. This holiday, she wanted something for herself.

As we spilled on to the quay with our baggage, my mother began the search for the appointed boatman while my father set off back through the crowded streets to find a car park. 'Does anyone know where I can find Tony Pengelly?' she called to men on boats, one stern eye on her three children: John, bookish and aloof at twelve; Paul, ten and naughty; and me, a timid seven-year-old wondering why we couldn't just have gone to Norfolk as usual, half the drive and a known end to the journey.

Everyone, we discovered, knew Tony Pengelly. A striking figure with his black beard, and a stuffed felt seagull sewn on to his red baseball cap, he was cheerful and impatient, with his boat *Nicola Jayne* already half full of people waiting for an afternoon trip to the island. When my mother confessed that we were incomplete, that my father was still parking the car, Tony headed out to sea without us, the boat disappearing as it turned at the mouth of the river.

We perched on the railings at the top of the steps, my mother silent, scanning the streets, not sure how long the crossing would take, how soon the boat might be back for us. Watching the sea to the left of us for boats, and the town behind for my father, none of us was ready for the plaintive shout straight ahead.

Looe is split into two towns, divided by historic rivalry and a broad river. Small boats run across the river at certain tides, but the ferry steps where passengers are collected and decanted are upriver from the flight we had settled at, and the tide was too far out for them to be working. Further up again, there is a bridge, but although my father must have driven over it, none of us had quite grasped that key element of the geography. As instructed, he had succeeded in finding a car park and parking the car, but then become quite disorientated, helpless on the west side of the river while we waited on the east.

Tony had returned from his trip, packed the other four of us and our luggage on to the boat, and run out of jokes by the time my father found his way round on foot. My mother still said nothing.

We set out to the harbour mouth, to the sea, and the air freshened. Over the low wooden side of the boat, I could trail my hand in the water, heavy as the boat cut into it. We left the shops behind, the lifeboat station, the beach; a white-painted rock marking the dangers on our right, and the pier, ending in its navigation lamp post, on our left. As you swing to the west, with a whole new shore at Hannafore opening up to one side, you don't easily notice the first sign of the island, an innocuous line of land sputtering out to rocks, and the bulk of it is sudden, a sleight of hand, your attention misdirected elsewhere.

It is a long, slow moment of dark green, from the first realisation to the full view. It is a turtle, a whale; a dark hump with a low spit of land – a finger, a toe, a tail – pointing eastwards. You can see white houses, a pale beach; and then trees, a 'No Landing' sign, and tiny people, perhaps, waiting on the beach to meet you.

Only Tony, the professional raconteur, and my brother Paul, who is incorrigible, broke the silence on the crossing, as my mother waited for her blood pressure to subside. My father's brain was brilliant, and his heart was full, but he was not a steady helpmeet. He was always, without exception, late. He stopped watches – he seemed to generate some odd kind of electricity which meant he could never wear one. He was always in love, and not always only with my mother. I adored him, then and always, but this was our last holiday with both our parents: the following year, my mother, my brothers and I came alone.

Thirty-five years later, as the boat cuts its way out over the harbour bar to open water, the island still takes us by surprise. For the first few minutes, it is invisible, hidden, no more than a possibility. We strain as always to catch the first glimpse of rock and salted grass stretching out into the sea, the white buildings, the dark hump of hill. The water is dark around us, but vivid with shadow and movement; ahead, where it meets a sandbank, it is a lucid pale green. Ernie, one-time trawlerman and Tony's winter boss, navigates us towards a sunset which transforms sky and sea into an ecstasy of light. 'Magical,' he says.

He is taking us home.

Chapter 2

Houses

---

*They need to recover
the innocence of rockpools, springwater, spray-filtered air.*

Chris Considine, *Setting Out*

When I first moved in with Patrick, home was a big, handsome house in an ugly part of south London, bought with the proceeds of happening to be in the right place at the right time in the world of IT. We had professional jobs – Patrick a sought-after technical guru, troubleshooting for huge companies across Europe, and me teaching at a smart school a few miles away – and solid middle-class aspirations. We wanted 2.4 children, and to move out of London before too long, but only to somewhere commutable, somewhere which would slot conveniently into our current lives. We looked sensibly round Kent and Sussex, and tried to summon up enthusiasm for the sleek villages with their excellent transport links and well-patronised gastropubs.

They were never able to spark in us any of the sense of relish, of relief, of freedom, that we felt when we crossed the Tamar for a weekend in Cornwall, and we turned our backs on common sense and bought instead a tiny house in Looe. We overbid wildly ('What happened,' I ask Patrick, years later, 'to all that money you used to have?' and he reminds me) because it was almost part of the island: this house on the mainland was the first foothold in Cornwall of the Atkins sisters, their shore base for forty years, and to me a place of glamour and mystery and desire. I'd wanted it forever, since the morning I was 12 and crossed from the island early in the morning of the third day of our fifth holiday there to pick up a delivery of many shrink-wrapped trays of dog and cat food from the store opposite the cottage. The 'helpers' of the already elderly sisters were inevitably drawn in to handling the heavier of the winter supplies, and I was thrilled to accompany Jack, the handsome 17-year-old I was secretly in love with, as he crossed to the mainland on this mission of brawn. Silent and joyful among the tins, I stood beside him on the quay waiting for our boat back out, with the fishing fleet returning up the river with the tide in the clean early light.

I can't remember a time before the island, before the summers with my family on its beaches and in its sea-pools. Our favourite place to be together was a miniature island, the size of a large back garden, which forms the last gasp of the land mass disappearing into the sea at the east. A narrow stone bridge links it, across a gulf of rock and water, to the rest of the island.

It was and is the domain of the gulls: herring gulls and black-backs, fulmars and terns, dotted with nests and corpses and impassable at breeding time. We found it early, in search of the much-vaunted natural rock swimming pool, and large parts of those holidays were spent in and out of the sea on what we christened Gull Island. On maps, prosaically, it is 'Little Island', but then the island as a whole is uncertain about its name, and is almost unique in the UK in having two official names: both St George's Island and Looe Island (as it always has been to the locals) are correct.

We stayed in the water as long as the tide was high enough, hauling out like seals as the sea retreated to search for cowrie shells on the minute beach and eat through Mother's store of Devon toffees. At low tide, Paul and I shored up the broken dam, built to keep water in the swimming pool, with stones and sand, while our mother swam length after length, undisturbed for once. John read *The Lord of the Rings* to me, unhurried over years, flat on his stomach on the beach with my head on his back and my thumb in my mouth. The quest to Mount Doom was delivered with a backdrop of seabirds' complaints and the sound of my mother's steady breaststroke through the rock-walled pool. I was quite content in the knowledge that I was no hero, no Aragorn or Frodo: I was Sam Gamgee, small and baffled and longing for the safety of the familiar. In the house moves and instability of our parents' divorce and our separate struggles through growing up, the island was our Shire.

As my brothers and I grew enough to become useful, and as the sisters' energy to maintain the cottages as holiday lets decreased, we gradually became part of the shifting army of helpers – students, conservationists, retirees – essential to the Atkinses for the backstage running of the island. As well as manning the café and attendant craft shop (Attie's pottery, Babs's polished stones), the helpers handled the boats, running a wooden trolley down for people to disembark, taking the 'landing fees', phoning Babs on the ancient field telephone from the top of the beach, and dispatching each group up the path for her to take over on the top lawn. We cut paths, made loosely saleable crafts from shells and pebbles, mowed lawns, repaired buildings, dug vegetable patches, made jam, and helped, to a greater or lesser extent, with all the day-to-day physical demands of the island, as well as the great set pieces of oil or coal deliveries, or bringing winter supplies from the distant mainland.

The sisters' little cottage in Looe was already uninhabitable at the time of that perfect morning trip ashore for the winter pet food: closed, mysterious for decades behind net curtains, full of old furniture; unloved as the frequency of the sisters' visits to the mainland sputtered out to nothing. At first, it had been an essential part of their island lives; baby sister Babs had lived there for 12 winters when she taught at the local school, while Attie sat out the island storms. Now, fifty years later, as Patrick and I moved in, and despite an overhaul by one of the island 'helpers', Jennie, in return for a few years' tenancy, which had ended shortly before Babs's death, it was once again empty and unloved.

When it became ours, we cosseted it. We took up the stone floor and tanked the damp walls, and persuaded the builders to spend a week stripping the ceiling downstairs back to old pine the colour of wheat. We spent joyous hours at reclamation yards, and when there was no floor downstairs in the cottage, we simply moved up, spending our time marooned on the bed, eating ham and crisp sandwiches and watching *Peep Show* on Patrick's laptop. Barry the builder's work is beautiful, doors and tiles perfectly scribed into the lumpy, sloping walls – and every time we visited Cornwall felt, for both of us, like coming home.

For a while, we tried to have the best of both worlds, and we were fortunate to have options. Selling the big London house would, we calculated, just about give us the money for a flat in London *and* a house in Cornwall, and we looked at a beautifully proportioned Georgian house outside Tideford and a four-square farmhouse at St Keyne; at a terrace in Tulse Hill, where the front of the building was coming off the back, and a pretty maisonette near Brockwell Park. None of the combinations was quite right, and we were nervous, too, about splitting our time. Would we only be in Cornwall for summer holidays and the odd weekend; would that be enough? Or might I move down and Patrick work from home part of the time – the concept of 'working from home' was not yet commonplace. What about the 2.4 children – in London, we were surrounded by friends, close to family: how would we cope in Cornwall, with none of that support network?

And what of my father, whom I still adored, living alone in Bedford, where I could visit him often and quite quickly from our London house? He was democratically 'Paddy' to everyone: colleagues, students, the foster children who lived with him, and Alison, his second wife, while they were together, and by now even to me. He was self-sufficient and well-known in the town, a distinctive figure in his deerstalker and raincoat, walking everywhere for twenty years as he gratefully turned his back on cars. They knew him at the coffee lounge in the Swan Hotel; at all the bookshops, of course; at the soup kitchen, where his utter openness to humanity made him much loved, easy to approach; at the churches of various denominations which he visited regularly – when he died, he had four separate funeral services. But he was never physically robust, and less so by this time, at 70. Patrick met him for the first time at his seventieth birthday, and I wish they had met sooner, the two hefty intellects with their frivolous edges; the two kindest men I have ever met. With my brothers abroad, I worried about basing myself 250 miles away – if anything went wrong for him, I would want to be on the spot.

I first met Patrick, briefly, at 19, and we both vividly remember the day. He had come to London to see his school friend Martin, my boyfriend at the time, and the three of us lunched solemnly at the Stockpot on Old Compton Street, where you could buy an improbable three-course lunch for a fiver. I didn't see him again until my early thirties, but we remembered each other. Reading the kind of magazine article which told me that 43 per cent of people meet their future spouse at university, I'd go through all the boys I could think of, ruling them out, until I got to Patrick and thought, yes . . . Eventually, with 13 years of water under the bridge, Martin arranged not a blind date, but perhaps a partially sighted one for us. 'I'll wear my shiniest armour,' Patrick emailed me beforehand, and I was suitably swept off my feet.

'If only,' we say sometimes, 'we'd got together when we first met!' The reality is that our youthful selves would have lasted barely five minutes together, but imagination insists: what adventures we could have had! And how easy, surely, it would have been for us to move on to the next step, and have a family. I was 32 when we finally did get together, and I knew the clock was ticking: I had seen the heartbreak of a couple of childless older friends, and infertility had become a bogeyman, one of the worst things I could imagine. Before I was 30, I had started canvassing gay male friends about co-parenting, so waiting for a year from that first date before persuading Patrick that now would be a good time to think about having a baby struck me as impressively restrained.

After six months, we bought a book on fertility and took its advice to see our doctor, who prescribed medication to galvanise my ageing eggs into action, and I crashed immediately into a depressive episode of a violence I hadn't experienced in ten years. It was the Easter term, and I had exam classes at GCSE, AS and A level with practical drama exams almost upon them, and written exams hard on their heels. I fell into sick leave, abandoning my students to overstretched colleagues: their results suffered, and I don't think they ever forgave me. I certainly couldn't forgive myself; I still sometimes wake in the night and am swamped by regret and guilt.

As I recovered – off the fertility drugs, and overseen by the uneasy alliance of an excellent psychiatrist and a ghastly 'crisis care' team on the High Road – my father had a fall. He fell hard, on to the pavement – a mini stroke, perhaps – and bruised his brain. We tucked him up for a short convalescence in our bedroom in London, but after he took himself back to his own house, we started to think perhaps his temper was worse, perhaps he was slightly more wobbly, perhaps his brain wasn't as sharp as it had been. 'He started from an unusually high level, intellectually,' his GP said, uneasily, when Paddy and I visited him together some time later, 'so it wasn't easy to spot things deteriorating': the realisation that, cognitively, he was no longer at full power seemed sudden.

The worry about Paddy's health, on top of that awful sense of betrayal from leaving my pupils just before their exams, was too much, and I handed in my notice, and left my teaching job at the end of that school year.

In the autumn, I tried a different drug, with the resulting depression slightly less acute than the first round. I drove regularly to visit my father, to take him to hospital appointments for memory tests and physical assessments, which havered about exact diagnoses: 'Some kind of dementia,' they said; 'perhaps Parkinson's?' On the way back from these trips, gridlocked on the South Circular, I was routinely consumed by terrible road rage, screaming into the unmoved box of the car.

By the New Year, our efforts had become focused on an imminent first round of IVF. We bought more books, and had several appointments with the top fertility guru of the times; I visited the clinic alone, too, again and again for acupuncture, Chinese breathing therapy, blood tests. We both had counselling; we were lucky to have a terrific consultant at a top London hospital. We saw a nutritionist, changed our diet – more seeds, less pork. I decided to try hypnotherapy in an attempt to start eating more vegetables.

I have never eaten vegetables, beyond a pasta sauce or an onion chopped small in a stew. My parents tried hard, years of counting five peas on to my plate, until they couldn't stand the sight of me swallowing them like pills, meal after meal, and gave up. I eat fruit, which has prevented scurvy, but my diet was not entirely ideal.

My hypnotherapist was a cheerful Irishwoman, who was breezy about me achieving my goal of eating vegetables willingly and without uncontrollable retching, in ten easy steps of visualisation. The ongoing building works outside her consultation room were something of a distraction, but I believed in her and felt buoyed by her confidence and good humour. Having settled me on her couch, chatting brightly away, she paused: the work was about to begin.

'Nooooow . . .' she intoned, 'you, and I, and everybody, Mary . . .' Was the silly voice a joke? Should I laugh? But no, this was Maureen's special hypnotherapy voice, and the process was hamstrung from that point by my inability to take it seriously. We had several sessions, and I tried to see the 'golden baaandages, wrapped in a soothing, healing balm' as a communicator of happy, safe feelings while I visualised broccoli, but I couldn't help the reaction that they'd just be sticky and unpleasant. We never got beyond step three, and I focused on eating more grapes and drinking less Diet Coke instead.

The egg collections, which followed weeks of needles, for acupuncture and for injecting hormones into my tummy, were oddly unfocused, sometimes trippy. The Cornish sea lapped at drugged daydreams; waking gradually from anaesthetic, Patrick holding my hand, I tried to explain.

'There were boats . . . going from A . . . to B . . .'

I could see the boats in the bay, between the shore and the island, but the urgency of it, the specificity, slipped away as I came to.

'Boats? Where are the boats going, Moo?'

'From A . . . to B . . .'

Patrick only smiled, but I knew there was something important in that dream, if only I could grasp it.

The hope is that once eggs and sperm have been harvested and introduced to each other, the eggs are fertilised and the cells divide and multiply day by day; the ideal is to get to five days after fertilisation, where the resulting 'blastocyst' embryo has a good chance of survival after transfer. Our single, lacklustre embryo had so little chance of survival that it was transferred to my womb on Day 3. I watched it on the scanner being delicately positioned, and felt sorry for it.

'Would it be better if you were on the island?' Patrick asked me once.

'Everything is always better on the island.' I had no doubt about this.

Often, then and now, when I can't sleep and am trying to still my mind, I walk myself around it. I step off the boat, on to the wooden trolley bridging the water between boat and shore, and then crunch on to the grey and white stones and shingle of Landing Beach. As the beach slopes up to the path, it becomes silver sand; sometimes there is samphire growing above the tide line, which is marked by a ribbon of seaweed inches deep and feet wide in stormy weather, a mere pinstripe in quiet summers. At the top of the beach, the old field telephone was attached to a tree where the woodland straggles down to the shoreline: we used to announce to the sisters the arrival of a boat by whirling wildly at the handle to make it ring at the house, panting up to the top of the beach after we'd pushed the boat off, to alert Babs and Attie before the visitors were upon them.

To your left, at the top of the beach, is the shingle path which is the main thoroughfare of the island, just wide enough for a quad bike. The first stretch of it is steep – an effort with a barrowload of luggage, or shopping. Then it plateaus, a path to the woodland on your right and then buildings: the tractor shed with its immense doors; a courtyard, between it and Attie's pottery, where they used to keep handcarts for hauling holidaymakers' luggage up from the boat; the dark and noisy generator room. To your left, a flat piece of grass, a precipitous drop at the far end to Jetty Beach, an apple tree. On both sides, fuchsia hedges with unshowy red flowers, and the dark, glossy green and hot pink of the escallonia.

The last building in this cluster, through a picket gate and up a straight garden path, is Smugglers Cottage. It was built, two centuries ago, with a generous walled garden but, by the end of the sisters' time, encroaching trees had shrunk the garden and darkened the cottage; ivy had swallowed the walls. I might picture it instead when Babs's friends lived in it, later on: a riot of rose and clematis on the front of the house, nasturtiums cascading down a step to the lawn, the medlar tree to the left and the cherry plum blossoming in the hedge to the right. There is a fig tree, with quantities of hard green fruit in the late summer, and when we were children there were half-wild blackcurrants in the garden, which I found too fiddly and too sharp to pilfer.

In my mind's walk, I leave Smugglers behind and carry on up the path, which becomes broader, the slope a little less steep. Periwinkles on the right, inland; sycamore on the left, covering the gash where the spring-water pump was torn out in the 1987 storms, and huge machinery brutalised the green cliff to replace and shore it up. The daffodil fields next – an irregular half of one of them is still glorious in the early spring with the white daffodil 'Beersheba' – then the magnificent globe artichoke, vegetable patches, a tall privet hedge, the house and Jetty Cottage coming into view as the island opens up to show the sea ahead, Little Island, the flagpole and the windblown grass. Babs used to meet the day visitors on the top lawn between the cottage and the house, sloping down to the bay window of what was then the café, and upwards to the archway through to the front door of Island House. Turn left along the near side of the lawn, as visitors do now, and the shingle patch squeezes you through the narrow gap between the door of Jetty Cottage and the cliff edge, then swings round above the jetty; the sea behind and in front of you now as you turn past the lower edge of the cottage, where the ox-eye daisies thrive, leaving the path down to Jetty Beach and the jetty behind you and to the left, and go past the helpers' huts, the Chalet, and right again up the hill.

If you carry straight on past the huts, you see Little Island ahead. The wild grass here, and at the very top of the island, meets your feet in springy cushions, unlike any other grassland I know. You can bounce your way across it, past the flagpole on your right, and suddenly steeply down to the little concrete bridge spanning a chasm in the rock – twenty feet across, perhaps, its iron handrail long rusted away – and up the other side to Little Island. A flat, bleak expanse of grass, half an acre at most, but if you go right across it and then bear left, there is – or was – a set of steps in stone and concrete down on to shingle, then sand: a perfect, tiny private bay. You need to go out to sea just a little in order to turn back to the rock swimming pool, dammed to be full even at low tide: my brother Paul once took a shortcut, jumped in from the rocks at the side and scraped himself on the jagged slate all the way down his back.

If you have resisted the call of Little Island, though, and press on up the hill, you have a glory of sea to your left and a hedge of escallonia to your right, running along the edge of the old croquet lawn, and the lawn to Island House. An old wooden gate, picturesque with lichen, would take you through to a path lined with purple hebe to your right and pale pink roses to your left, up to the back of the house. Continuing on the main path, though, you now have a choice of a broader path to the left or a narrower one to the right, along the edge of the woodland: years ago, the right-hand path was the only way uphill, steep and still and penned in by bramble thickets on one side and sycamore on the other. Persevere, puffing, and you come out at the top of the hill, on to open grass, a couple of disputed, vaguely ecclesiastical stones at your feet, and ahead of you beyond Looe, the Hore Stone, where the mainland falls into the sea to the west: the sunsets are dazzling here.

Turning to the right again to loop back around, and treading cautiously in dry weather on the wind-flattened grass, you are looking at Hannafore, the western edge of the island wood on your right, Dunker Point jutting out below you and to your left, High Cove a short swim round from there. You follow the path into North Mead, where previous owners used to grow potatoes, a standing stone incongruous in the middle of the bracken. A modest slab of rock the height of a small person, it links, perhaps, to a ley line: the disputed idea of an imaginary line linking, in pre-history, important sites for religious, or astronomical, or trade reasons. Another now stands in the garden of Island House: Attie was once sent an old map by a mysterious Surrey clergyman, with X marking the spot, and her dowsing rods went wild at the site, but nothing was uncovered until a dig many years later probed more deeply and found just the great stone. Perhaps it once, dragon-like, guarded the treasure Attie and the clergyman assumed the map would lead to, but if so it was looted long ago.

Below the stone, almost at the edge of the cliff, is the low bench to your right where Gus and Sheila used to sit and watch the water traffic in the 'Island Roads' between the island and Hannafore. Once, before the plates of the planet began to shift, the island would have been part of the mainland, and this is the closest point, at which they must have been linked; there is evidence of great drowned forests linking the two. Perhaps, later, there was a causeway, and the island was still just a suburb of Looe, a grassy protuberance only, until tree-planting began in the nineteenth century, and sycamore took hold, the woods now giving an entirely different character to acres of the island.

You go into the wood through the path from North Mead, and the light dims. There are paths through the wood to the chapel site, a zigzag up from this end, a straighter path where Jack Proffitt-White built wood-edged steps to take you straight upwards: both emerge, now through tidy gates and stiles, to take you back up to the top of the island. Stay on the low path, though, and you find you are walking above the main beach, past the NO LANDING sign, and out into a clearing where a cherry tree blossoms fire-coloured in the spring, back to the tractor shed, and the main path.

By the time I have walked myself around with my mind's eye, my heart rate has slowed.

Patrick and I were on a short holiday in Norfolk, after our first IVF pregnancy test had returned a negative result, when my father phoned. 'I've been listening to a programme on Radio 4,' he announced, 'about vascular dementia. I think I might have it.' This was almost the only time he appeared to have lucid awareness of the disintegration of the extraordinary intellect which had been such a key part of his identity; I suppose that was a blessing of sorts. He was more taken up with physical pains, and although I stocked his freezer with home-made one-man fish pies and portions of chicken soup, he was eating very little. He was increasingly vague, though, and the doctors were confident that he was just *forgetting* to eat; perhaps he was also a little depressed? The GP diligently sent him for various tests – endoscopies showed nothing; blood tests were a little out, perhaps, but nothing could be diagnosed.

The settled order of our London lives – secure jobs, steady socialising, parents minding their own business – had changed, and perhaps this was one of the factors which caused Patrick to reconsider his working life. An exceptionally able and hard-working IT 'architect', he travelled extensively for work before I met him, in a different country every week, moving on to a big job in a huge oil company shortly after our relationship began. On the side, at the point where I met him, he had just finished a psychology degree, bought a Persian restaurant which he and his business partner were turning round from the edge of bankruptcy, and invested in a Spanish technology company which gave me a delightful visit to Barcelona.

Perhaps it was unsurprising then that when the opportunity arose for an even bigger job at his company, he felt oddly uninspired. He was beginning to realise that a nine-to-five existence, and life in a big corporation with its stultifying hierarchies and procedures, might not be for him. Importantly, too, he no longer felt the urge to make money for its own sake – there was security in his big London house, and money in the bank.

Over curries or beers, and over some years, Patrick had found himself discussing escape routes with his friend Justin, equally out of love with his job publishing a 'business to business' magazine. Before I met Patrick, the two of them had already put together a business plan to sell the software which Justin developed in order to run his business, but with technology not sufficiently developed to allow for what's now known as cloud hosting, such a business wasn't financially viable. It wasn't quite, though, an idea they could let go of.

As Patrick dreamed of being his own boss, I missed employment. Although there were down sides to teaching – exam specifications, parents, a three-hour round-trip commute from south London – I had loved much of my job. The spark of an idea, the surprise of achievement, lighting in a child who thought she couldn't 'do drama', or that exam results were all that mattered. I loved the relationships, the collaboration, the trust. I hadn't realised, either, how much a job contributes to your sense of identity, and I felt lost without it.

I applied to be an examiner for an A-level theatre paper: a stretching occupation for a few weeks, a nice bit of pocket money, in a gap before our second round of IVF. The job would start with a couple of days where all markers for the paper met in a room near Holborn, with the senior examiners on hand to direct and advise, before we were let loose with a bunch of papers and a mark scheme. The night before the first meeting, I rang Paddy to say good night: he had become more erratic, recently, and I was trying to work out a schedule whereby either I or his partner, Jackie, could stay with him for the great majority of the time. Until this month of marking was out of the way, we were relying on phone calls and the good offices of his sister, who lived a couple of miles away from him.

'I'm ready!' he said.

'Ready . . . ?'

'For you to take me to the hospital!'

An appointment was in place for the next morning, to which my aunt was detailed to take him, and Paddy, who had perhaps slept for a while in the afternoon, was now convinced it was 9 a.m. on Wednesday, not 9 p.m. on Tuesday. He was distressed by the time I managed to persuade him that he should be going to bed, not into town, and putting the phone down was miserable.

My phone rang an hour into the next morning's meeting: Paddy had vanished.

Ringing the warden at the sheltered flats where he now lived, then my aunt, friends, his favourite place for coffee, I missed most of my meeting but tracked my father down, finally, in hospital. He had fallen again and been taken in, and as he was still complaining of pains in his stomach, they had scheduled an ultrasound the next day.

An uncomfortable doctor told us about the pancreatic cancer, the metastasising which had already taken place, the inadvisability of treatment, but wouldn't give us much of an idea of how long Paddy might have. I was determined that at least he would have it with us, and he didn't protest. I drove him home, we summoned Jackie, and sat him down to tell him he was going to die. 'I knew there was something wrong,' he nodded, grimly Spike Milligan.

Having sent him and Jackie up to bed, Patrick phoned his oncologist brother-in-law and we talked him through the doctor's report. How long were we likely to have, we wanted to know. It was June: would he be with us for Christmas, say?

'Think how fast he's deteriorated so far,' Johnny said, gently.

'My brother John's coming over for the summer in a couple of days,' I thought aloud, 'but Paul's in Australia. Should I make him get on a plane?'

'Yes,' said Johnny, and I couldn't be more grateful.

Paul arrived a few days later, and both my mother and Paddy's second wife, Alison, came to visit; my stepsister Lucy arrived from a gap year in Greece. After a week in our house, Paddy suffered a heart attack and was taken to hospital: he spent just a few days there, lost, before a Macmillan nurse came and whisked him off to a hospice – 'a lot of people go home again,' she told us, but Paddy didn't. His brother and sister came to visit him, and between us, my brothers, Jackie and I were with him all the time for the four days he was there. John and Paul, Patrick and I sat with him through a long night three days after our second wedding anniversary, and held his hands as he died, not long after the sun came up.

That round, there were no embryos at all, and for our third, and last, a year later, just one, as 'poor quality' as the first. We watched again as it went into my womb, and held each other's hands. I had planned to go to the island with my brother John and his family, over for another summer, but I stayed in London instead, waiting quietly for a fortnight. When we saw our lovely consultant for the last time, she told us, 'There really is no point in trying again.'

We no longer had a real reason to stay in London, and we put the house on the market.

Caught between the loss of my old family and any new one, I longed for the island, for any contact with it. It called to me as it called to Ross, Attie, my mother: every time we went to stay in Looe, we walked round to the east side of the river, and peered at the little blackboard where Tim, the boatman of the time, wrote up his trips to the island as Tony, Dick and Dave had done before him. But often we found 'No trips till Tuesday', or an empty board. Tim, like most of the boatmen, was well past retirement age and had other interests to enjoy: he was in France with his caravan, we'd hear; at a motorcycle rally; helping out at the British Legion tent.

'Is there *anyone* else?' we begged Tony. It was 25 years by this time since Tony had been the island boatman, though even after parting with his own boat, the *Nicola Jayne*, he continued as the island postman – employed by the post office to make a fortnightly delivery – to the end of the sisters' lives and beyond, bringing groceries and prescriptions and mail-order gadgets along with the post. He came in their boat while it was still sound, but although he bought another of his own then, *Fore Girls*, she was a little too big to land on the island, and he enlisted another boatman to take him out with the post.

'Ernie Curtis,' he told us. 'Look out for him on the ferry – a dark blue boat.'

I identified Ernie ferrying passengers across the river, his dark hair standing out among the grey heads of the ferrymen. I thought he looked serious and unapproachable, and was afraid of being barked at, until I saw him one day standing in his boat, moored at the side of the river, holding a loaf of bread. 'Where's my crow to?' he demanded of the sky. Ducks dashed towards him to compete for the pieces of Spar's or Palfrey's finest wholemeal (he won't let the birds have white bread); they flowered from nowhere like sea anemones around *Pania*, always foiled by the quick necks of the swans. A gull launched from the 'Do not feed the gulls' sign, to dive-bomb them all. 'He's a West Looer,' Ernie explained, cryptically, looking to the top of the mast as the hoarse-voiced crow was conjured. 'There you are, my boy!' – and the black bird descended to take a slice from his fingers, and was gone.

Although we crossed with Ernie once or twice, boatman politics are delicate and we couldn't undermine even an absent Tim too often. Our hours there were short and visits rare. The island remained for the most part tantalising, just out of reach on the horizon.

But I came to Cornwall often, unemployed and unsettled: no longer anchored to London, its hospitals, the M1, which had taken me to my father in Bedford. We were ready at last to commit to a full-time life in Cornwall, and I viewed dozens of houses in the east of the county, around Looe and Liskeard and Launceston, and became obsessed with slate floors and space to keep a pig. Some of the houses were plain wrong; some we disagreed on, when Patrick came with me for a second viewing; some offers fell through. With our cottage in Looe – too tiny by indulgent modern standards for the long term, but charming as a stopgap – we could afford not to rush; we could wait for the perfect property.

Our London house took a year to sell, in the early bite of the recession, but we continued to make plans. We could live anywhere now, and full-time, not only because of what we had lost, but because the advent of broadband meant that Patrick and Justin could finally deliver their product over the web, and so their business model was viable at last. Their first formal meeting as co-directors of a new company took place at our kitchen table in London a few weeks before we left the city behind us.

The island was by this time owned by the Cornwall Wildlife Trust. The Atkins sisters had famously rejected fabulous offers for the place, and had left it in its entirety to the body they felt shared their values. Our relationship with the island changed, of course, with the change in management, but we had been able to maintain contact, to visit when we could find a boatman, to stay for the odd night. Jon, the Wildlife Trust's warden, now lived on the island full-time, and he put up with our attempts at 'helping' with bits of gardening or other island maintenance on a couple of our trips, although his standards were disconcertingly high. Wiry, strong, determined but measured, he looked right on the island – smarter than the helpers of old, in Wildlife Trust branded sweatshirts and steel-toecapped boots, a few years older than us but immeasurably fitter.

In the summer we were gearing up to leave London, Jon was planning a summer break to cycle around France for a couple of weeks with his partner, Claire. We were delighted to be included on the list of possible island-sitters they emailed in May, to look after the place for a fortnight in late June – meeting day visitors from the boat, keeping the impressive vegetable gardens going, and tackling some of the endless jobs of island maintenance. 'It's a bit like Hamilton Island (without the blog or £80k),' they emailed: the 'best job in the world' of caretaking Hamilton

Island, in the Great Barrier Reef, was being advertised around the same time. Other invitees were proper conservation people, so although we replied straight away to say we would love to island-sit, we thought we were very unlikely to be chosen. What we did have in our favour was the ability to go away for a fortnight – by this time, Patrick was pretty much on gardening leave at his job – at short notice, and presumably the better-qualified people couldn't: we were ecstatic to receive the thumbs-up. 'We are most pleased to offer you the position of Island Sitters! (Looe not Hamilton . . .)'

The timing was improbably fortunate. With house, jobs, family and future in a state of such flux, the island offered unmatchable sanctuary, a perfect balance of safety and stimulation. The prospect of being a cog in the wheel of its day-to-day life, as I hadn't been since the volunteering holidays of the Atkinses' time, comforted me immensely, and was a draw, too, for Patrick, with his zest for any new challenge. We had just enough time to fit in the requisite course on 'Emergency and Basic First Aid' – the main message was 'if in doubt, call an ambulance', which wasn't quite the rugged, hands-on guidance I'd been hoping for – and an induction day with Jon and Claire to give us more 'basic first aid' instruction for the generator, the spring-water pump, and the vegetable gardens and greenhouses, before we were alone in Jetty Cottage, where I had spent the earliest and most magical of my childhood island holidays.

*

Jetty Cottage is perhaps the oldest of the three stone buildings on the island, all of which are rendered and painted white, with bright blue woodwork. A century before we first visited, it was a barn with a false floor under which smuggled contraband was concealed; fifty years later, a music room. In 1979, the big room was a café, a craft shop, with our accommodation in a warren of little rooms added on to, or partitioned off from, the barn. My brothers and I slept in a room of old iron bedsteads and cobalt blue bedspreads sparking with nylon static, and we ate our tinned meals in a lean-to with only a narrow shingle path and a bramble hedge between us and the sea.

Just up the hill from the cottage, past Babs's greenhouse, round the corner, up a step, and squeezing through a narrow passage between a shed and the helpers' loo, is Island House, where the sisters lived: designed to look imposing, to deter potential intruders, its many elevations and high roof conceal the modest two-up, two-down inside. For most of the sisters' time, the house was out of bounds – not only to children, but increasingly to all the various kinds of island visitors: holidaymakers, volunteers, personal friends. To Babs and Attie, in their seventies when we first arrived, it was a fortress whose entrance was increasingly defended. On Day 1 of our first family holiday, Babs gave us strict instructions on where to find the appropriate water for drinking and cooking, washing up and flushing the loo, and after that our interaction with the house should be, she made clear, as far as possible at an end. We daily weighed up the benefits of a fresh ice block for the cool box, from the island's only freezer, against the brashness needed to knock at the sisters' door at the time of the evening when they had been charming throngs of visitors through a long, hot day and were finally relaxing into sherry and salad.

Tony brought day trippers by the dozen, sometimes the hundred, in those days, working any tide in his shallow-draughted boat, the *Nicola Jayne*. Babs met them all in groups on the top lawn, with the white house rearing up behind, to tell them with enthusiasm undimmed as the hours passed the same stories of boats and whales, cannonballs and treasure. Ushering them past the house and into the café, she handed each batch deftly on to some of the diverse summer army of helpers, and hurried back out for the next boatload. The visitors sat in the cool barn, or on the shingled space outside under the palm trees, while refreshments were prepared in a tiny, blisteringly hot kitchen squeezed in behind a partition, where sweating students produced stainless-steel pots of tea with matching jugs of powdered milk.

Running errands as a child, I had my first encounters with Island House: calling in to collect scones, fresh from the oven, for the café. It was thrilling to penetrate the forbidden territory as far as the doorway into the kitchen, just across the hall from the front door, sneaking glances along the passageway over piles of books and demijohns of home-made wine.

The helpers themselves lived in a pair of garden sheds with

bunk beds, below the lawns of the two houses and near the top of the path which sloped down to the jetty – or if you were lucky, in the luxury accommodation of the Chalet, a two-bedroomed aluminium refugee from a holiday park, at the end of the row of huts. When Patrick and I came to island-sit thirty years on, the better shed had been repurposed as a bird hide, and the other had simply collapsed, plank by plank, into the vegetation, but the Chalet was still standing, shifting slightly in the winter storms, patched up each year. The emptiness of it was arresting, reduced to a shed: the tiny, sunny kitchen where you looked out on a bright day over glittering water towards Little Island, where as a teenager I once saw through the window the hallucinatory vision of a deer which had swum across from the mainland, now just a tumbledown cupboard. Yet walking past at night, I like to think you can still sometimes catch a glow of candlelight through the sitting-room window as the helpers there, Kath or Ro or Katie, sit up after the generator has gone off.

The sisters, in their fortress, were all-powerful, fascinating, alarming. Attie, the elder sister, and author of bestseller *We Bought an Island* – signed copies available in the craft shop – was larger than Babs, more aloof, increasingly only sporadically involved in wider island life. They sported matching grey perms and glasses, but Attie's shrewd eyes were magnified behind thicker lenses, and her mood was always unpredictable. Babs, ten years younger, and not long retired from her teaching career, seemed to us the practical one, who handled bookings for helpers and holidaymakers and met everyone who set foot here. Attie, the nickname from a wartime stint in the WRNS, had been the driving force behind their move to the island in the sixties: ten or twenty or thirty years later, she still wielded powerful charm and was given to expansive passions.

Joan, a long-time helper, brisk and competent with short white hair and some expertise as a gardener, was left in charge one day while the sisters ventured ashore for the regular hairdressing appointment they still kept up in the seventies and eighties. She was entrusted with a tray of seedlings to plant out in the vegetable patch; they had been nurtured through their babyhood in the big greenhouse, tucked in between the house and the café, and were to be moved into a sunny, sheltered space behind the privet hedge.

When Babs and Attie returned, cheerful and coiffed, they caught up with Joan at the vegetable plot to inspect her handiwork, and the peace exploded.

'We don't plant them there!' Attie howled. 'They'll be far too shaded. They won't grow there! That's not where I said!'

'Well, OK,' Joan agreed, 'but I thought perhaps the brassicas might be better—'

'That is NOT where we plant brassicas!' Attie's voice had risen to a hysterical pitch, and we eavesdroppers scuttled away from the scanty protection of the hedge as she gathered momentum. Dismissed, as Attie put it, as 'the wrong age, the wrong sex and in the wrong income bracket' to take on the island, the sisters could never stand any semblance of being told what to do, of having their hard-won judgements contradicted. By the time we sauntered casually back past the veg patch, as if we hadn't heard a thing, Tony had already been summoned and poor Joan banished, exiled, after years of island summers, never to return.

When one of Attie's favourite helpers, Dave, set the island on fire, experimenting one sunny day with a mirror on a grassy slope, she simply roared with laughter and poured him a whisky – but she was less fond of women, and a capricious ruler of her kingdom. She did not accept challenges to her hard-won supremacy: when my mother, a well-regarded poet with many publications and prizes to her name, produced a small book of island-based poems, dedicated to the sisters, they maintained a stony silence until she finally asked what they thought. 'Not a very happy choice,' was the frosty response. There was only space for one writer on the island.

Less dramatically, but steadily as the sisters' energy to charm, motivate and organise faded, the number of helpers declined. Within a decade of our first family visit in 1979, the vegetable gardens of Joan's disgrace had shrunk to token patches among the bramble. When we came for our summer stint of island-sitting, two more decades later, the gardens around the house had become taller than I am with a wildness of bramble and ivy: the escallonia I remembered pruning with my mother, along the path to the washing line, was almost vanquished. Escallonia dies decisively; the dead stems become the most brittle sticks, bone-dry and edged in bone-white. The trim hebe hedge along the path to the lower gate sprawled for yards, stretching and gasping for sunlight beyond the encroaching scrub.

I didn't go right into Island House until some years after the death of both sisters – and then, even though I was there by invitation, the house half cleared by the Trust and the sisters' friends, I couldn't stop looking guiltily over my shoulder. Babs and Attie guarded their privacy so fiercely that the sense of transgression was almost overwhelming: I had barely been further than the doorstep in their lifetimes or since their deaths, not even daring to peer through the windows.

Miss Havisham would have felt at home in the house as it had become, although the decay was that of old age and harsh weather, rather than her vicious despair. Curtains hung at the windows, but they had rotted from the hems upwards. Paint and paper were tearing off the walls, and the floors were littered with plaster. Holes in the floorboards showed where the rats had chewed their way into shelter. The place was full of books and dust and difficulty, a lost battle of the sisters' resolute old age.

The Cornwall Wildlife Trust, on inheriting the island, had begun to clear the house, burning furniture pinpricked with woodworm, preserving boxes full of dusty papers and photographs, moving the endless books into one upstairs room.

By the time Patrick and I arrived to stay in Jetty Cottage for our holiday cover, Island House was largely open to the public. Downstairs, where the floors were more or less safe, the Trust had set up a sort of museum through which visitors could walk: along the hall, past the roped-off kitchen and the roped-off stairs, into the big, sunny sitting room and out on to the far lawn. The Atkinses' collection of communication devices was arrayed in the kitchen: a history of ship-to-shore radios and walkie-talkies, a Motorola analogue bag phone which Patrick identified with interest. I recognised the field telephone, with its whirly handle, still in the wooden box which kept the weather off it at the top of the beach, from where we could use it to tell the answering sister how many visitors were on their way.

The Trust set out kitchen gadgets and utensils too, on the shelves and on long Formica tables, picturesquely battered, rusted, vintage. In the sitting room, two armchairs were pulled up to the fireplace, with an album of old photographs beside them; the sisters' pictures and ornaments still adorned the room. Their books were laid out for sale in here too, and home-made jam and Wildlife Trust calendars and notelets. Bird skulls and bones waited on the dusty cupboard in the hall.

It was no longer a living house, but an idea of one, frozen in an unspecified moment, fascinating. I found it disturbing too, and sad, and felt shifty every time I walked into it, in this incarnation. We had visited it a few times on our hard-won trips to the island in those years when we were still living in

London but starting to dream of escape, and had sighed over the great slate flagstones of the kitchen floor: 'This is EXACTLY what we want in our house,' I told Patrick every time. Sometimes, back on the mainland, over jugs of sangria in the East Looe wine bar or pints in the sunny garden of the Admiral Boscarn, we daydreamed giddily about living in Island House and bringing it back to life. By the end of a session, Patrick was always geared up – 'Let's put a proposal to the Trust!' – but by the time the hangover kicked in and we were back to London, to work, to reality, we both realised it was impractical: how would we earn a living, keep an eye on my father, and send the children to school?

That June, island-sitting, those arguments had dissolved, and the scented air was balmy. Patrick was astonished by the warmth, and quite uncharacteristically took off his jumper. He relished meeting the boat, pumping water and fettling the generator. Having flirted half-heartedly with the island over the last few years, on this trip he fell suddenly and unexpectedly in love. Sitting in the sunshine outside Jetty Cottage, under the flowering palm trees, a new conviction grew, and he said decisively, 'We should do it. Let's call the Trust.'

Chapter 3
The Sisters

---

the island fading behind us, mist
on mist, paler and smaller and then   not there.

Chris Considine, *Crossing*

Babs and Attie had no intention of leaving the island, the greater part of their identity for forty years and more, while they had the strength of will to battle on. But as Attie approached 90, she fell, badly, outside the house which had been for so long their refuge, though by now, with its privations, it was almost an enemy. Her bad leg wouldn't heal, and the house is unforgiving for the very infirm.

No boat could approach the island in the February sea, but the air ambulance landed on the croquet lawn, the one flat part of this undulating island, so that Attie could be stretchered on board. Tethered on her back, she couldn't watch the island zooming out below her, or hear the gulls above the alien roar of the aircraft. She could make no kind of farewell to the place which was a settled, immutable thing inside her, and she knew she would die if she left it.

Her funeral was two weeks later, at the little church on the quay. The night before it, just arrived from London, I walked along the sea wall which curves from Pennyland around to White Rock, sheltering a small shingle beach at low tide, where the totemic statue of Nelson the Seal watches the harbour. From there it loops back in and runs along Hannafore, up beyond the coastguard hut, with a clear view of the island along its final strait. In the days before health and safety, one could walk, with a little inventiveness, all the way round its curves. The dark path consoled me a little, after a day of grief and confusion, leaving my overnight bag on the bus and tracking it for hours, my funeral outfit inside, through the wilds of Croydon, sobbing in the street. An unsettled twenty-something, I was afraid that nothing could be the same now: Babs would leave, visitors would no longer be welcome. The fixed point of my childhood had slipped.

Babs came in last to the church, which was packed with mourners and spectators spilling out into the street, walking slowly up the aisle with her dog Lucy, the sight of them catching the throat. We staggered through 'Jerusalem', which for Attie meant the island: those 'mountains green' would be an overstatement for the island's gentle slopes, but legend told her that the child Christ was brought there by Joseph of Arimathea on his fabled tin-trading trip to England.

We moved up to the cold, wet graveyard on the hill for 'dust to dust, ashes to ashes'.

Afterwards, old friends gathered in the hotel across the road. Tony was distraught.

'She'd always give me a drop of whisky, when I came out in the winter. "Keep you warm on your way back to Looe," she'd say, slipping it to me on the boat. I don't drink whisky, but I never said.'

Attie's fearsome passions were entirely positive where Tony was concerned, both sisters' devotion to him, and his to them, enduring throughout their lives. By the time Attie died, he had had a steady job ashore for years, no longer delivering the oil and coal and gas, the vast winter supplies of dog food and gin, or the endless boatloads of visitors and helpers to the island; but every weekend he still put out to sea on the sisters' boat (the *Amazon*, of course) to deliver groceries and post.

'How will Miss Atkins manage,' he fretted, 'all on her own?' Babs was always Miss Atkins to him, since she taught him at the school in Looe. At Attie's funeral, 'Miss Atkins' was only a year away from 80, and without her sister, her partner, her galvanising inspiration. No one could find an answer for Tony.

It had taken us time to become friendly, then affectionate, with the sisters. John, my oldest brother, started the process by augmenting, from his early teens, family holidays with a second annual trip to the island as a helper, serving tea in a bow tie and boasting to us about his prowess with a Chillington hoe. I followed suit: John heroically let me come with him when I was 13, and after that I brought myself, finding my way to the island with my underdeveloped sense of direction, on three trains and across London ('west on the Circle Line, towards the West Country . . . east coming home, for East Anglia,' my mother explained), to come alone for Easter trips, returning a second time with my mother in the summer.

We began to find we were among the favoured ones invited to join the sisters, when we arrived for our week or fortnight, for coffee or elderflower champagne; there were parties with other helpers too, around a barbecue of mackerel from a friendly boatman, or a showcase of the latest gadget (ice-cream maker, fondue kit, SodaStream). The sisters and their idiosyncrasies became, as my brothers and I negotiated our uneasy way through our increasingly split lives, a blessedly fixed point, as familiar, essential and taken for granted as our own grandparents. As a string of house moves began, our visits to the island were a constant, a talisman.

Around the big table in the café, even though the numbers of visitors and helpers dwindled through the eighties and nineties along with the sisters' energy, there were still parties – smaller ones, but with salads full of flowers, and dandelion wine, stirring renditions of 'The Sun Has Got His Hat On', or pen-and-paper games. For Hamilton's first birthday, there was a cake made of dog food, with a carrot for a candle. They always had dogs – gentlemanly Lucky, thieving Emma, faithless Lucy – but Hamilton, a gangling black-and-white collie cross, was my favourite, barking at wheelbarrows and jumping up at everyone, as tall as a man, on his hind legs. He could sometimes be persuaded to come down to the beach with us, dashing delightedly along the shingle but sprinting back to the house the moment he heard the doorbell being rung, his signal to come home.

In the summer after Attie's death, there were no parties. I came to stay as usual, with my school friend Katie who used to come with me on my independent teenage trips, to her mother's bafflement: 'If you want to work in a garden for no money, there's plenty for you to do here!' We found Babs as tough and dignified as ever, until the evening we took it into our heads to persuade Katie's boyfriend to swim out from the mainland and join us a day early. After all, Katie had previously succeeded in wading over at the morning low tide, and Simon was a strong swimmer, a sporty Oxford blue; and that stretch of water looked so short, until we watched from the far side of it as he stepped into it in the poor light, a larky version of Ross twenty years later, vanishing again and again as the sea and the sky grew dark.

Hysterical with relief as he landed, finally, in front of us, we made excuses to each other as we avoided passing Babs's door – 'It's late . . . we don't want to worry her . . .' – and were bundling him into emergency dry clothes and running round with hot food, hoping to have got away with it all, until, 'Fireworks!' Katie reported, looking out of the window. 'No – oh no – it's flares.'

Sprinting, shoeless in our hurry, down the shingle path to the beach where Katie had seen the lights, we were terrified that what must be a search by the lifeboat would reach Babs before we could head them off. Men in oilskins turned their torches to scrutinise us as we screeched to a halt at the bottom of the path.

'We've had a report of someone going into the sea at Hannafore – a member of the public called the coastguard.'

'Oh, I'm so sorry,' we babbled.

'It's my boyfriend, he's come to see me –'

'You see, she waded this morning and we thought –'

'We didn't realise –'

'We're really sorry –'

'Where is he?'

'He's just up there, in the –'

'In the hut, where we're staying, just up –'

'We'll need to see him.'

'Oh, but he's just . . . he was really cold, and –'

'He's wearing her clothes and –'

'He's all right, honestly.'

'He's absolutely fine –'

'We'll need to see him. We can come up with you.'

'Oh no!'

'No . . .'

'You see, we haven't actually told Babs that he's –'

'We wouldn't want to disturb her . . .'

'We'll need to see him.'

We look at each other.

'We'll go and get him,' and after a painful dash back up the path, we presented Simon to the lifeboat crew's satisfaction. They let us off remarkably gently, and we made the largest donation we could scrape together to the RNLI as soon as we got home.

Babs, though, was more put out than I'd ever seen her, and although she didn't scold us, or exile us, her sense of hurt and ours of vulnerability were painfully evident.

'We didn't want to disturb you,' we muttered, but we knew it was a feeble excuse; she was never early to bed.

'We just didn't think.'

'But I like the men,' she said sadly. I think of this years later, of how much she'd have loved Patrick. We had left it too late, though, for Simon to charm her. 'All of Looe will be talking about it,' she fretted, and there was nothing we could say.

Babs, usually safe in her fastness, could feel suddenly vulnerable here alone, and decades later, Patrick and I feel the same unease: at once worryingly remote from and worryingly near to the shore. When I walk down to the generator shed at night, a trip I avoid as often as I possibly can, I am on edge for fear of the dark, the shadows, the ghosts; but Jon the warden, joined by his girlfriend Claire, fear intruders, that one day they will come face to face with an aggressive trespasser in the generator shed. When they take action against a fishing boat, netting illegally in the inshore waters at night for mackerel, pollack, bass, by shining their torches at the water to scare away the fish, it's all too clear that the men on board know where they live, and Jon locks the door that night, as we never normally do, and sleeps with a poker by the bed. For Babs, completely alone in the house for the first time in her eightieth year, our demonstration of how easily someone could come here without her knowledge was bound to frighten her.

Those night-time netters, an ongoing threat around the Cornish coast, and suddenly evident in the bay a couple of years into our island tenure, represent serious organised crime of a kind we hadn't expected to find here. They are often unnoticed because they work at night, but one summer morning Patrick leaves at first light to catch a train and phones me, back in bed and half asleep again, from the boat.

'There's a net across the beach,' he tells me. 'Ernie says it needs moving or boats are going to get tangled up in it. Tell Jon.'

It's hard to take this too seriously: there is always net on the beach. It's washed up as regularly as seaweed; heavy chunks of it stirred in with sand by winter storms are as immovable as if they're growing straight from the bedrock. Fragments of nylon net hide in the weed we take up as fertiliser for the potatoes, and appear incongruously in our vegetable beds when the plant life has rotted away. I know better, though, than to contradict Ernie, and I knock apologetically at Jon's door on my way down to the beach.

I don't see it at first. The left-hand side of the beach is clear – but as I reach the point where sea meets land, one of the birds perched on the water doesn't fly away. Squinting, short-sighted, I become aware of a line stretching away on either side of it: the top of the net. The bird, I think, is a young cormorant: long-necked, almost black, but not quite the size of an adult bird. I love the cormorants, who inhabit the far side of the island; they seem happy to co-exist with other birds, with us, unlike the black-backed gulls, which pick off the mallards' ducklings from the water like sweets, and swear and bully their way around the island. The cormorants stand quietly on their rocks, wings spread to dry, after efficient fishing trips in the quieter, wilder parts of the sea where boats don't go.

This bird, I realise, is trapped. I have no idea how to free it, how to handle it, and it is several yards away from the shore, so I run back up the path to find knives and chest waders, to update Jon on his way down. By the time I return to the beach, perhaps five minutes later, the bird is no longer alone; there are half a dozen, caught in a line on top of the water, unable to move. I wade in and start to pull the line where I can see it, a little further along from them; I want to bring them close enough to the shore to have a clear purchase on the ground, to be able to disentangle them without finding myself underwater. I hope too that by starting further along the net I might alarm them less, but of course they panic as they come closer to me, and the dangerous shore.

Jon and Claire join me, with knives and gardening gloves. The net is a modern nylon one, the spaces between strands just big enough for a bird to stick its head through. They are all impossibly tangled, trussed by their struggles in the net, fighting to keep their heads above water. Claire and I, chest deep, develop a system: we reach first for the beak, with a gloved hand, to hold it shut, because the instinct of the bird is of course to stab and peck and see us off, to fight the predator for survival, and we can't safely cut them free while they are thrashing about in attack. This leaves one hand to hack through the strands of the net, trying to work out what to cut to free the bird, trying to get them out fast before they drown. Jon holds up the rope to which the net is attached, and reaches to supply an extra hand to whichever of us needs it more. Some of the cormorants are easier to cut free than others, but all of them take several minutes, the net twisted around wings, feet and necks. One is already dead.

The last bird is badly caught, the net cutting deeply into one wing; I can't see how it can survive, or even move, with its injuries, but as soon as its wing is free, it starts to wriggle, and shoots off underwater as quickly as its fellows. There's a temptation to 'rescue' the birds, to take them up to an outhouse, feed them, contain them while they recuperate, but of course the trauma alone would probably kill them.

With the cormorants released, and the dead one cut out from the net and carried up the beach to be buried above the high-water mark, we set to work hauling in the rest of the net. We have a frustrating fight: at first it pulls out easily, then it sticks on the east beach, but between the three of us and the tractor we manage to free it enough to haul it out of the water, and start to cut out the fish – wrasse, pollack, mullet – caught along the rope.

As we heave, we notice a small boat just off the beach, a small, dark boat we don't recognise, carrying two darkly dressed figures. They seem to be helping us; they are shifting the net. Claire calls out to them, and they suddenly shoot off to the east.

We realise that they were cutting the net free from their boat, that they are almost certainly the culprits. There are rules about how close to land you can cast a net, what depth of water there needs to be above it, to prevent the deaths of birds and seals and dolphins, but you can make a lot of money out of the fish you catch through illegal netting. This net has evidently been cast at night but been caught on the rocks; the dawn operation to cut it free has been interrupted by Patrick's early departure.

We phone the coastguard, and we phone Ernie, who we know will be around the river, and ask him to watch for the boat coming in, but it changes direction and shoots off to Millendreath, a few miles along the coast, where it's spotted being loaded hurriedly on to a trailer, which then disappears.

Grimly, we return to the net. We find it's stretched right round to Little Island, nearly half of the island's mile-long circumference. We haul and cut, throwing live fish back into the water; we're happy to eat fish, but couldn't possibly get through the number here, and the wrasse are not good to eat, so we work as quickly as possible to return those which are still straining for fish-air. When they regain the water, they rest briefly near the bottom, exhausted, gills pumping, before slowly starting to move bodies and fins to mobilise into safer, deeper water. Those which are slower to revive are deposited back on the sand by the incoming tide; if they are still moving, we throw them back to gasp again for water.

We arm ourselves with photographs, and phone numbers for the Fisheries and the local harbour master, but when the nice man from the Fisheries comes to talk to us, he is not optimistic. 'We think we know them,' he tells us, 'but it's very hard to prove whether it's a drift or a fixed net.' There is more latitude and less danger if the net is drifting in open water behind a boat. 'They make hundreds of thousands, the people in charge, and the fines if they *are* caught are just a business expense.' I'm reminded of the ongoing battle, centuries ago, between Customs and smugglers: it is so easy to be on the side of the latter, now that smugglers and pirates have been positioned so romantically, light-heartedly, in popular culture, but the reality must have been brutal and bitter on both sides.

Jon is right to worry about the consequences when he encounters the boat again, a night or two later, and scares the fish off with his torch, but his regular night-time patrols put off these netters, at least in these waters, and the cormorants have one less threat to their quiet lives.

It is easy to feel safe on the island, securely isolated from humanity and properly respectful of the impersonal menaces of the sea, but you are exposed, too, vulnerable, a sitting duck. Perhaps Attie was right, and the island rejects where it needs to, because the men in the dark-coloured boat never come ashore, and when Ross knocks at the door, it doesn't occur to us to feel anything other than a friendly interest. 'Weren't you scared?' people ask later, but really, we weren't even surprised. If we'd taken Simon up to the house, Babs would have raised an eyebrow and given him a whisky. We can bear the known.

When her friends Gus and Sheila visited early in the spring, a year after Attie's death and at the end of Babs's first winter alone, they asked her how the winter had been, and she burst into tears. Babs was not given to emotional outbursts; the only time I ever saw her in thrall to emotion was years earlier, when her dog Emma barrelled into the sea after an escaped mink, and Babs stood on the beach picturing the creature's sharp teeth and desperation to survive and shrieked and shrieked for Emma to come back. It was the dogs that kept her going over that lonely winter, she told Gus and Sheila: Hamilton, who by now was inseparable from her and walked backwards in front of her wherever she went, barking infuriatingly; and Lucy, sleek and dark as a small seal, who had none of Hamilton's fidelity and would trot back to the mainland with strangers at a very low tide.

Sheila – when Babs and Attie talked about her, she was always 'our Sheila', as distinct from other island regulars 'Sheila the Healer' and 'Sheila the Dealer' – was the greatest of the Atkinses' favourites. The first time I met her, she was hoeing onions, and I felt slightly put out – partly because I didn't know how to use a hoe, and partly because if I were only here for a day, as she was, it wouldn't occur to me to do anything so useful. My school friend Katie, now in early adulthood, agreed that Sheila's husband Gus – always good-tempered, humming his jaunty way around the island – was our ideal man. Everything he did was done thoroughly, steadily and without fuss. I follow his method of planting potatoes today: you break the ground up first, and then collect seaweed from the beach. You can then dig the trench, lining it with newspaper, followed by your home-made compost and, last, the seaweed, before the potatoes finally go in. 'Beautiful!' Ernie reminds me now, every time he sees a slew of seaweed on the beach. 'My brother always used it for his potatoes – like flour, they were.'

Gus and Sheila, both practical and impulsive as they comforted Babs, formed a plan which transformed her life and death. Still youthful in their sixties, they moved into the decaying Smugglers Cottage for six months, 'with four dogs, two cats and a parrot!' Babs told us. They made a new kitchen in the dilapidated old bedroom, pushed back the bramble and ivy from their garden, planted hollies, camellias, crocus and nasturtiums. They put a woodburner into the ugly fireplace there, warming and cheering the neglected cottage. Practical, cheerful, sociable, they were as ideal as new companions could be. 'You're almost as good as Attie for shopping!' Babs told Sheila once, as they pored over catalogues for plants, gadgets, Tupperware, in a muddle of dogs and cups of tea, and she gratefully relinquished the twice-daily tyranny of the generator to Gus, with many other small responsibilities and tasks.

'The only thing is,' Sheila confided to us on a visit, 'she won't let us in the house. She's burned through another gas poker – she must leave it in the Aga all the time. It can't be working properly, but she won't let Gus in to have a look. We could make her so much more comfortable . . .'

The initial six-month stay expanded, running on into that winter and then into the next, and when Babs was diagnosed with leukaemia six years after Attie's death, they committed to staying with her for as long as she needed them.

I read the email telling me of Babs's illness in the staff room at my first job, in the gap between lessons and prep. It was, perhaps still is, an Enid Blyton school in the same way that the island gave us Enid Blyton holidays: ponies clattering through the courtyard at lunchtime, the games mistress's yellow Labrador sunning himself in a doorway, dormitories and midnight escapades. But this news brought an end to another part of my childhood. Sheila was set to accompany Babs to the hospital at Plymouth for regular blood transfusions, but Babs was in her eighties by now and, essentially, she was dying.

I spent a week on the island in the early autumn that year, alone but for the three island inhabitants, the old pattern of work abandoned entirely. I think Sheila was glad to have someone to talk to, and I was glad to take part in the rituals of Babs's days: gin and orange, carefully buttled by Gus, before lunch, and whisky before supper, the three of us joining her, still firmly in a chair in the old café room, to talk the hours away. Babs was still upright and engaged, still keen for news of my family and our lives. Gus and Sheila's commitment to her had delivered her from a long, slow decline ashore, weeks or months in hospital, and as her physical health deteriorated, she retained colossal dignity.

She had already protected the future of the island. After Attie's death, there were offers, as there had been over the years, of vast sums from businesspeople who thought a hotel or theme park would do rather well here. Both sisters always scorned these; even the National Trust, who they had approached for advice in their early days, would be unsuitable: 'If the National Trust owned the island,' Attie was advised by a representative, 'they would have to commercialise it to make it pay . . . in order to bring in enough income to pay a warden, his wife and staff . . . He could not see it as a viable project.' Babs took advice, from her friend and confidant Sir John Trelawny, and from her solicitor,

Mr Browning, and decided in the end that the Cornwall Wildlife Trust shared her and Attie's ethos sufficiently for her to feel that theirs would be the safest hands. Legalities notwithstanding, arrangements were made quite quickly for the Trust to take possession of the island, up to a point, straight away, paying Babs a peppercorn rent of a case of Laphroaig per year.

There were not many cases to buy.

The Trust made gentle changes, bringing across a small flock of Hebridean sheep, black, horned and hardy, to roam the cliffs and manage the scrub. They put up a stock fence across the spine of the island, behind the Chalet, along the edge of the wood and down to a gate at the side of North Mead, though sometimes the sheep make a foray straight down a sloping rock face on to the main beach, where they huddle incongruously on the shingle. They began a slow process, increasingly purposeful when Jon took over as warden, of pushing back the brambles and ivy which had started to swallow the island as the sisters aged and the helpers dwindled; of bringing buildings back into use, planting trees.

Jon is part of a world which must be the future for the island, a world of organised volunteers and serious knowledge, an offspring of sixties communes and the student helpers who gilded the island in the seventies. The world takes climate change and conservation seriously now, and getting the kind of job which Jon has here, in an organisation which must once have been considered a bunch of cranks, takes as much commitment, skill, and years of unpaid work as the most lucrative and sought-after City jobs with their impossible internships.

In our first full-time summer on the island, our friend Jason visits, bringing tiny, striped beetroot; tender carrots; sweet peas; and a hint of credibility, because Patrick and I know we lack the passion, the knowledge and the sheer physical fitness of Jon, Claire and the others in the Trust and beyond, and we are outside that world. Jason, though, can hold a man-to-man conversation with Jon about trees, what and where to plant: the hollies and hazels, the maple and the oak, at the edge of the wood or along a wilder fence line. He has turned his back on the bars of Soho, standing ovations in the theatres of the West End ('Where was I going to go after that?' he asks), to become part of a community based in a stunning, ramshackle stately home in Devon. He lives in a caravan in the grounds, and plants thousands of trees there: he sings with the other residents every day, has trained himself to be open, tolerant, sunny. He is a shining exponent of the kind of commitment to eco-living which Patrick and I know we'll never manage.

He is also impossibly handsome, and Sheila, in her late seventies, and my nephew Finbarr, not quite four, marvel at him and all his charm. He leaves us and the country to save the daisy trees in St Helena, to protect that island from the plant invasion which is making it a monoculture, to help it to become healthy and balanced and able to sustain itself.

Our island life is more chaotic, less focused, than that of Jon or Claire or Jason. We have something to bring to our house, but the wilding land needs a skilled hand and physical stamina. It has thrived under the subsistence farmers of the nineteenth century, the paid staff of the early twentieth and the volunteers of the late; and now has guardians who can combine the expertise, the dedication, the energy of them all.

It was those guardians, the Wildlife Trust, who we approached five years after Babs's death, to ask about her abandoned house. 'Money talks,' people are still scoffing, years later, with half an idea that there are people who have bought their way into living in Island House, that due process has not been observed, but really talking talks: no one else went to the Trust with a plan for the empty house. Technology was only just ready for us to be able to work remotely from the island, because without the pensions of Babs and Attie, Gus and Sheila, or the direct employment in the service of the island of Jon and Claire, the problem of earning a living here rules it out as a possibility for most.

We didn't expect them to say yes, but when we phoned Callum, Jon's boss at the Trust, he didn't immediately say no. When we phoned Jon, he told us, resignedly, 'I wondered how long it would take you.' By this time, he had been on the island for five years, and Claire had recently joined him full-time to become the warden's assistant, leaving behind a teaching career to become a fount of information here on butterflies and seals.

Like Jon, she is a little older than us, but fitter, better turned out; tall and willowy in contrast to the more cuddly proportions Sheila and I share, although Gus and Patrick assure us that we are their cup of tea. Between them, Jon and Claire have the island running smoothly, the museum-house a part of that, and perhaps aren't entirely delighted about our plans: no one opts to live on an island nature reserve with the expectation of new neighbours in a house only a few steps away from their own.

With the response from Callum and Jon no worse than neutral, though, we travelled three months later to the Trust's rural headquarters, further down into Cornwall, for a meeting with both of them and with Callum's boss. There were questions, of course: were we planning to have children? Did we really need to bring the cats? There were grey areas – what would our involvement be with the Trust's work; what would our role be over the winter? The essence of the proposal, though, remained the same throughout: for us to renovate the house, sympathetically (it is unlisted) and with as much use of 'green' technology as possible, in return for a long lease. To this essential outline, there seemed to our continued surprise to be continued agreement. I kept wondering what Babs and Attie would have thought: of their house being lived in by other people, of those other people being me and my husband. I wondered if Babs would haunt us.

In her last weeks, Babs's world becomes tiny. It is the bed and the windowsill, which she feels rather than sees; the space on the other side of the window is lost to her. She has held out for as long as she can, because in her generation dignity and restraint count for more than comfort. She has kept her kind companions at bay, and carried on with the gas poker smouldering indefinitely, inflammably, in the temperamental Aga, while the curtains rot at the windows. When the sheets had gone too far, she slept in blankets, and Hamilton took most of those.

He seems to understand that he sleeps on the floor now, but he never leaves her. After a decade of walking backwards in front of her, keeping constant watch, barking his protection, there is nothing for him to say now that she barely leaves her bed. She has been made comfortable in Jetty Cottage, refusing to the last to let anyone in her house; she has been persuaded into clean sheets and soft quilts. Sheila brings meals and helps her to the bathroom; Gus mixes her gin and orange at bedtime, now that whisky seems too harsh. Their miniature dogs come with them, but she doesn't see them any more.

There are no more blood transfusions now, and no visitors over the last, slow winter except professionals. As spring arrives, the nurse sees that death is finally coming, and Sheila is prepared when she finds Babs still and cool one morning, neatly under her sheets, with the marvel of her life behind her. She lies now in the daffodil field, and Hamilton, who was silent after her death and buried at her feet within a year, knows that she is safe.

*

Babs's March funeral, and her burial at the top of the field which slopes down towards Jetty Beach, was attended only by lifeboatmen, an emotional Tony, and Gus and Sheila, but many people wanted to make their goodbyes and so a memorial service was arranged for the summer. Her great-nephew Colin, almost her closest relative now, was set to speak about her and his family to play music. Sir John Trelawny, whose family had owned the island for centuries, and to whom she had left the tiny outcrop of Gull Island in recognition both of the history and of his very present friendship, was also going to speak, among others, including me.

I wish I had asked Babs more about her life; I wish I had listened more carefully when she spoke, and written everything down. Once, having supper in the Chalet with me and Katie, she talked to us about time she spent in Germany just after the war, part of the reconstruction effort, teaching the children of the military: how could we have been, how *can* we be, so casual about these buried, incredible fragments of lives, so confident in our own memories, in the ongoing accessibility of those whose lives are vanishing?

On a beautiful, blazing day, in the bigger church on the east side of the town, next to a room glorious with island photographs, I talked about teaching. I talked about Babs's career, and the esteem and affection in which hundreds of pupils still held her. I mentioned, haltingly, that time in Germany, her quiet courage among unthinkable devastation. I talked about what she taught me: about courage, dignity, perseverance. 'No one sees her when they all go home,' Sheila used to say, when someone mentioned how tireless Babs was at 85, meeting boatload after boatload with her tales of cannon and whale.

Words and tea, old faces and emptiness. Sheila suggested we could spend the night on the island – my old friend Katie, our friend Ingela and I – and we snatched the unexpected gift. On the grass outside the old chalet, with our disposable barbecue in the evening sun, I was able finally to forget about my stumbling, fumbling for the right words, about the dizzying number of people clamouring, in life and death, for Babs's attention. The sweetness of the island air contained us, and Babs was everywhere: in her greenhouse, the old café, the generator shed, the beach, and there was no more demand for her to be tireless.

Babs, who would never have dreamed of talking about her own feelings or trespassing on other people's, encountered me one afternoon when I was perhaps 12, on the same sheltered patch of grass which is a popular lookout point to check for the boat coming out of the harbour.

'Any sign of him?' she asked.

'I don't think so . . . I thought that one might be him, but I think it's the wrong blue.'

After a little pause, Babs asked, 'Is it very difficult, now your parents are apart?'

I shuffled and muttered, 'It's a bit sad.'

'Do you think they might ever get back together?'

I shook my head, and we both gazed firmly out to sea. Tentatively, Babs offered:

'I hope you don't mind me asking, but I do feel like a grandmother towards you.'

And she smiled at me, and walked softly back towards the house.

Chapter 4

Wedding

After Babs died, I wondered if my relationship with the island would die too. It was Gus and Sheila, staying on in Smugglers Cottage under the dispensation made in Babs's will, who continued to welcome me there: we had become friends through the concerns and grief of Babs's illness and death, and as Sheila upheld the sisters' traditions of letter-writing, we kept in touch.

When I got together with Patrick, less than a year after Babs's death, it was inevitable that our first holiday together would be on the island. Although Patrick never looked much like anyone's idea of an IT wizard, neither expensively suited nor coolly Conversed, his extraordinary hair black and wildly vigorous, he was a member of a slicker, far-off world. The sisters would have been oblivious to that; they would simply have recognised his skill and loved him, and his genius for electronics, engines, machines.

Gus and Sheila welcomed him with the equanimity with which they greeted the many visitors, dull or odd or curious, who tramped past their gate. They made him tea, and chatted to him gently about dogs and boatmen and weather, and he sat in their damp cottage admiring Gus's beard, falling in love with their basset hound, Cluny, with her engaging grin and waving tail. He managed to his surprise to survive for three days without internet or phone. He couldn't believe how damp everything was, and how primitive. He couldn't get over the quiet.

Returning to London, he swapped his gas-guzzling Mercedes for a Prius, the ground-breaking electric hybrid of the day, and started to think about buying a wind turbine.

When my proposal of marriage, a year later, came with the condition that the wedding had to be on the island, he was not surprised.

We had three months to plan for a safe summer wedding date. It was a ridiculous project, the timescales far too tight; no one had married on the island before and there were all sorts of licences and permits to organise, the Trust's permission to seek. They agreed, perhaps wearily, in principle, and we managed to get Jetty Cottage – the smugglers' old barn, the Atkinses' café – licensed as a wedding venue. With the wedding date in July, we were hoping for good weather for the celebrations afterwards: to barbecue mackerel from Pengelly's, sausages from the farm shop; to drink toast after toast of the champagne we could still afford then. July should be safe, too, for the boat, but when we arrived in Looe the day before the wedding, paperwork signed off with days to spare, we met Tim the boatman on the quayside to be told that the weather was far too rough to cross.

'You see?' He gesticulated around us. 'I'll show you! Get in the boat.' Out at the harbour bar, there was a faint movement of water. Another boat came towards us from the open sea. 'No good, is it?' Tim sought corroboration. 'Well . . .' the other boatman hedged. Patrick and I looked at each other and Tim steered triumphantly back to the safety of the river, point made.

Patrick's best man was his brother William – energetic, excitable, charming – and the two of them took charge, two men of business with a problem to solve.

'A helicopter!' Willy started to warm up. 'We'll get a helicopter. Who was that bloke Victoria used to go out with, in the RAF?'

The council of war took place to the music of gulls, sunlit outside a café near the water. Holidaymakers around us debated flavours of ice cream, or the respective merits of shark or mackerel fishing, but Patrick and William were oblivious.

'How hard can it be? We'll charter one! How many people can they take?'

We'd only sent Patrick's hand-drawn invitations to our immediate families and a couple of friends, so in total there were about twenty of us to transport. My brother Paul – who with flight delays spent 54 hours travelling from Australia and just under 50 in England, in making this trip to our wedding – was the last to arrive: he reached Looe that breakfast time and went straight for the bananas, of which Australia was suffering a national shortage. This was to be his first trip to the island, if we ever got there, since he was 16, when he'd spent an ill-advised three weeks there alone and afterwards chose holiday destinations with accessible pubs and people. It would be our father's first visit since he left my mother 25 years ago, travelling now – just two years, as it turned out, before his death – with his third (almost-) wife and the teenage daughter of his second, my stepsister Lucy. Patrick's sister Victoria brought the wedding cake she'd made, and her three children, all under five. All our guests in their own ways put themselves out to be here.

Tony, the boatman of our childhood, walked past mid conference, and we appealed to him for help. He looked worried. 'I'll do what I can . . .' he offered, doubtfully, and perhaps it was Tony who galvanised the lifeboat coxswain, who galvanised Tim. I was appalled when I saw the lifeboatman, with his prematurely white hair and splendid red trousers: the same man who'd insisted we had to show him the body when Katie's illicit Leander swam across ten years before.

Somehow, by the end of the day, we had two boatmen lined up for the morning and no helicopter was required. Tim even agreed to take us out that night as we'd originally planned, so that we could wake up on the island on the day of our wedding.

Jon the warden put up a tent for us on the croquet lawn, surrounded with candles. Patrick woke at dawn, bringing champagne to the tent and opening its door to a dazzling sunrise: both the eve and the day of my wedding blaze with light.

Patrick was on the beach in a vivid sou'wester as the tide came in to meet two boatloads of the most beautifully dressed people the island has seen for fifty years, and a small pirate at the prow of the first boat, while I put on silk stockings and Bond Street shoes and felt surprised.

Sheila filled one of the old glass battery containers with flowers, and picked little wild roses, which my mother worked into my hair while Katie applied make-up, as alien as the stockings for island life, and Amanda, my oldest friend, managed the bonhomie and photographs. After promising the bright-haired registrars that we would nurture our marriage whatever the weather, we sang Attie's favourite 'Jerusalem' at the chapel site at the top of the island, dizzy with sun.

My father-in-law, in a white cassock, blessed our marriage and wept for Patrick's mother, ten years dead and looking down proudly on her son. Martin, the old friend who had originally introduced us, read with his unforced actor's voice the predictable passage about faith, hope and love, which I read again at my father's funeral, years later. Patrick's sister gave me a beautiful row of family pearls in time for the wedding, but I wore as planned the rough-cut malachite which Amanda's mother had given me. She had died a fortnight before; Amanda's father was a last-minute guest, to be consoled by his friend my brother John, and Amanda wore gold shoes which both the lost mothers would have loved.

Small children chased each other in and out of Jon's tent on the lawn. Paul barbecued mackerel with an Australian nonchalance. Lucy, in a quiet moment with my father, who was struggling in the heat, told him, 'I love you, Daddy,' and everyone had shed their smartness and given themselves up to the sun by the time Victoria's penguin-topped cake was cut. Gathered on the beach at the end of the day, watching the boats gliding towards us over the shimmering sea, we were a motley collection, and even the little pirate had lost his hat.

The house stood behind us as we made speeches on the lawn, in unoccupied limbo, and never entered our wedding-day dreams for the future. It was the backdrop, though, its familiar bulk framing the sunny scenes on the lower lawn. We barely noticed it, the white paint greening and flaking on the walls, the window frames rotten, the rooms abandoned, but it was waiting for us.

Three years later, at our summit with the Wildlife Trust, we undertook to repair or replace the roof, the guttering, the fascia boards; to replace almost every window in the house; to supply hot and cold water to kitchen and bathroom; to install woodburners for heating, and solar panels; to completely rewire; to supply a lavatory, basin and two sinks, and to renovate the enamel bath; to install a Calor Gas cooker; investigate subsidence; treat woodworm; re-plaster; and to redecorate every inch of the house, inside and outside. We would need to have this finished within six months, and every nail, screw and paintbrush would have to come over from the mainland. Workmen would be limited by tides and, of course, weather, which can be unpredictable even in the summer.

The lease we negotiated was for a set term, twenty-odd years, with the house reverting to the Trust at the end of that time. If we chose to leave before the term was at an end, we wouldn't get any recompense, and subletting was not allowed. Battered by the three years since our wedding, the failures of lives, the critical thing for us was to take on the project: part of me wondered as we fixed the details if we'd renovate the house and then leave – if we couldn't manage to earn a living from Patrick's new business, as the recession bit, or cope with the solitude of island life, the dependence on each other. It seemed grandiose to think of ourselves as custodians for the house, as the scions of stately homes sometimes do, but we were quite clear that it would never belong to us, that the journey would be the reward.

The day after that big meeting with Jon and his bosses, four months after our summer caretaking stint, we piggybacked on a boatload of seal surveyors to head out to the island. It was

October, already later in the year than I'd ever been there: brilliantly sunny but cold in the shade of the trees, and wet underfoot. We exulted over coffee with Gus and Sheila, who were still living there. We walked up to the house with Jon and Claire, making plans to empty it of thousands of books, stacked upstairs, of furniture in various states of decay. We viewed the place, illuminated by the glittering winter sun, with new and astonished eyes, thinking: ours.

Chapter 5

Winter Trial

Needing to know what's behind, beneath.
There are legends, rumours, a rough sketch
with X marking the spot.

Chris Considine, *Scratching the Surface*

Jon offered us Jetty Cottage for a trial run, that coming winter. He and Claire were tied to the island only for part of the year, and in the winter they travelled: Cuba, Argentina, Sri Lanka. Gus and Sheila fed the sheep and kept an eye on storm damage; if we survived our trial month, and signed the lease we'd discussed, we would be winter backup for them, though we cautiously committed to one winter at a time.

We needed to prove ourselves first. I'd never stayed on the island in winter: Babs and Attie simply closed down in September, and didn't see anyone other than Tony until Easter, when the transition back to society was evidently agonising. At 16, Katie and I came as the first helpers, at the start of the Easter holidays. We travelled on the overnight coach to Liskeard, caught the first train to Looe, and turned up at 8 a.m. to the boat we expected to take us to the island, to discover that Babs and Attie weren't ready for us, or couldn't quite face the demands of other people, and we found ourselves stranded ashore for the day. We had no money for cafés and knew no one in Looe, so we went down to the small beach at Hannafore and huddled under our coats. I fell asleep, after the uncomfortable night on the coach, and it was only Katie who saw the embarrassed mother pulling her child away, whispering fiercely, 'Leave the homeless person alone.'

Patrick and I had barely even been in a boat in the winter sea, though at the quayside a few days before our first Christmas as a married couple, a couple of years back, we'd found Tony and Ernie about to leave for the island, loaded with Gus and Sheila's Christmas delivery of mail and groceries, and had been delighted to hop aboard. The sky was lightening from the east as the boat grumbled its way out to sea, and the old joy rose as the island slid into view. That day was pale with light, the sea reflecting the morning, the air cold and clear. The winter island, new to us then, was as bright and beautiful as on our wedding day.

The day our winter trial was due to start, though, was wet and windy: heavy weather. 'What do you think?' we asked Ernie. We asked this question a lot. It means: do you think the sea is calm enough, the tide high enough, the light good enough – and sometimes: are you in the mood to take your boat out to the island, with us in it, for a sum of money which is arrived at through the most tortuous reasoning, and probably often wrong?

It was late November by this time, and the weather was uncertain. Ernie, who had agreed to take us across for this winter stint, decided that we should phone Gus and Sheila: 'They'll know.' We raised them on the phone, and 'No,' he said, and 'No . . .' and 'No – no, no,' and we went back crestfallen to the Looe cottage with another day to wait.

The cottage was crammed with belongings from Patrick's big London house, the Edwardian pile he'd bought not long before we met. It always felt like his house, I never warmed to it, and while the cottage was a delightful, indulgent plaything and escape, the idea of our first proper house together, Island House – always assuming we could cope with the trial month – was thrilling.

When we finally crossed, with food, bedding, clothes and essentials for a month all packed up in orange Lambeth Council recycling sacks, it was pouring with rain. It had always been a grind to get stuff up from the boat – all those summers with a fortnight's worth of tins in a rucksack – but this was of a different order, and we were very wet by the end of it.

But dear Gus had lit the woodburner in the Jetty Cottage bunk room, which had been knocked through from the two little bedrooms where we used to stay as a family and furnished with handsome, sturdy bunks hand-made by Jon. We set up our wilting air mattress between them – we would need each other for warmth – and ate soup gazing into the fire.

Gus and Sheila were occupied that evening, and perplexed for the next few days, by Edward. He travelled out on the boat with us, chaperoned by Gus and Sheila's son Nick and heaved up on to the jetty by Nick from below and Patrick from above. Babs's companions shared with her a passion for dogs, and had five at one stage in their tiny cottage, when they absorbed Hamilton and Lucy after Babs's death. But that November, they found themselves without one, and were given Edward by the basset-hound breeders they'd known for some time. He was four years old, and no one else seemed to want him.

Edward was not quite what anyone expected. He was more than lugubrious; he was positively sad. Overweight, he lumbered around in a miasma of glumness; he smelt stale. He had not expected to move at this time of life, and was silently appalled by the boat, the cottage, the sea air, but all his unexpressed confusion and alarm became focused, implacably, on Gus.

Gus not only looked the picture of a mild-mannered and cheerful old gentleman, he really was the most sweet-natured person I've ever met, humming his way through life. Was it his hat, or his beard which was so threatening; his stick, or the torch with which he looked for Edward at night, to bring him out of the garden vegetation and back to warmth and comfort? Edward wouldn't accept food from him, and if Gus was anywhere near when he was eating, he checked constantly over his shoulder; if Gus came too close, he ran.

He ran as only a basset hound can: ungainly, ridiculous, weighty. He took to walking round and round the outside of the cottage, round and round and round, wearing a path in the undergrowth. Used to basset hounds of a sunny disposition – Patrick's favourite, Cluny; her predecessor, Wally, the first on the island; Fothersgill back in north Cornwall – Sheila phoned the breeders for advice. They'd known Edward all his life, and doubtless knew what they were letting Gus and Sheila in for; they might have been able to offer wisdom from the front line of animal psychology whereby Edward's oddities could be dissolved with some simple training.

They suggested sage. The cottage was probably haunted, they said: scatter sage all round the outside.

Gus had an odd sort of dream that night. He heard scratching and scrabbling, insistent at the end of the bed. The rats had departed, in a huge Wildlife Trust cull. The cat was out. Edward was in a miserable heap at Sheila's side of the bed. As Gus fell asleep, he realised: monkeys! It sounds like monkeys! His and Sheila's cottage was not far from the outhouse where a group of monkeys once lived, the darlings of the Whitehouses, who sold the island to Babs and Attie in the sixties. Going ashore on a winter's day, concerned that their pets might be too cold, they left them with an oil stove and returned to find the monkeys had knocked it over and died in the fire.

Perhaps it was the monkeys Edward feared, or perhaps it was Wally, whom Gus once watched walk all the way across the beach to join Sheila, before he remembered the dog was dead. Perhaps it was whatever was abroad the night Gus woke to feel Sheila's hand on his face: something terrible had happened, an explosion perhaps; her hand was gently feeling all over his face to make sure it was still in one piece – but he turned over to find her fast asleep beside him.

Although Edward came to love her, jumping unnervingly up on his short, unstable legs when she came back into the garden from, perhaps, the washing line opposite, Sheila missed the three little dogs, with their silky blonde coats, who had come to the island with them and Wally. As Edward's lonely path around the cottage grew deeper, a few months after his arrival and ours, I concluded that everyone needed a puppy. With some difficulty, I tracked down a litter of the precise cross-breed Gus and Sheila had had before: a chihuahua and Yorkshire terrier mix known in these days of designer breeds as a Chorkie. We met the parents and the puppies as advertised, and brought home Tolly.

Tolly turned into a wiry, fox-like dog, a tough little terrier nothing like the soft-haired dogs we expected, but he was devoted to his new owners, and he certainly saved Edward. Instead of pacing the garden at night, Edward would now lie in front of the fire washing Tolly's ears, or chase him adoringly in and out of chair legs in the little sitting room. He lost weight and lightened in colour; he began to walk the island with his tail up, to greet everyone amiably, sometimes with pleasure.

Except Gus.

Island winters are, we had always gathered, exceptionally balmy: no frost, no snow, daffodils at Christmas. Jon's edict that we should go easy on the fuel for the woodburner in the main room of Jetty Cottage (luxuriously carpeted in anticipation of further weddings) should therefore, we thought, cause us no hardship.

We were cold for a month. We wore multiple jumpers and multiple socks, and Patrick worked with a blanket wrapped round him and a hot-water bottle on his feet. We held out for as long as possible every day before lighting the woodburner, chain-drinking tea to keep warm; the room never got above nine degrees. We discovered winter Pimm's, which is drunk warm with apple juice, and sipped it with whimpers of pleasure at the end of the working day.

The wind, though, came as no surprise. The sisters, we knew, relished the island's inaccessibility in winter: they ordered cases of gin and whisky in the autumn, the hundreds of tins of dog and cat food I'd once helped to fetch, and a supply of books, and tucked themselves up, surrounded by their animals, for six months by their temperamental Aga. They were once cut off so completely for the weeks leading up to Christmas that a helicopter landed with a mercy drop of festive supplies, delivered by Father Christmas to the croquet lawn. For our winter trial, day after day as November turned to December, the weather was as wild as that Christmas must have been, the palm trees dripping and clicking, the sea too grey to look at. I knew it would be sensible to be out and active during the day, but I couldn't face the weather: the idea that going out would make me warm seemed preposterous, and I hunched indoors boiling kettles and reading through novels in the kitchen: as this was a glass lean-to, it was the warmest spot if there was any, watery, sunshine.

A few days into our winter stay, we found Sheila, for once, worried by the weather. She had a hospital appointment which she was anxious to keep; the previous week she'd had some symptoms alarming enough to call out the lifeboat to take her to the doctor, who referred her on. 'They were so kind,' she told us of the crew; 'one of them held my hand all the way over.'

Calling out the lifeboat had always struck me as exciting, a great adventure, but we had come to learn that the point where you can justify it is rarely an entertaining place to be.

Ernie had agreed in principle to take us ashore for Sheila's appointment, but the forecast was not good. Waiting for an early-morning phone conference, Gus and Sheila faced defeat: 'He won't be coming now.' But Ernie always came out when he possibly could: he phoned at the last minute, and with a modicum of encouragement – 'Give it a go!' Patrick suggested – out he came.

Ernie's boat was higher-sided than the slightly smaller boats which had served the island for the last few decades or more. Getting aboard was not straightforward at any time, and that morning it was hair-raising. The trolley, a metal version of the old planks on wheels, and so sturdy that half of it had to be cut off after it was delivered, as no one could move it, was repositioned several times so that the boat could safely come alongside it. Ernie passed out a fish box, which we perched upside down on top of the trolley to give us a better chance of climbing aboard, but it floated away every time the trolley was moved. Meanwhile, the paddle with which Ernie was desperately trying to prevent the boat running aground suddenly slipped from his hands and began to float off itself.

I'd had some scrambles to get aboard, but as Patrick, soaking wet from retrieving Ernie's paddle, pushed Sheila from behind and I pulled from within the boat, I started to realise the dangers in winter crossings: to a person with any degree of frailty; and to Ernie's livelihood, the boat. I started to understand why the sisters became so very reclusive as they aged, faced with the unstable trolley into the unstable boat; how seriously Sheila had had to weigh up her health worries against the mental uncertainty, the physical difficulty, of achieving a winter crossing. And although the hospital's verdict set her mind at rest, we didn't get home that night: unreliable phone signals meant we missed the daylight, missed the tide, and spent the night at the invaluable cottage in Looe, the next crossing postponed for a day.

We become fond of *Pania*, with her rich dark blue hull, an image of her namesake – an 'ocean maiden' of New Zealand, where Ernie's brother lives – just below the tiller. She, like an increasing number of the small open boats which bring to the island the seal surveyors, the day visitors, the guests to our wedding, is fibreglass, and although they look very similar to the boats I remember from childhood – open, no more than twenty foot, carrying not more than a dozen people on a bench which runs along the edge of the boat on either side – I rather mourn those little wooden boats, which were 'clinker built' with overlapping planks, a design centuries old. In the Atkinses' day, with boatloads of tourists coming perhaps every half an hour and 'beach duty', along with 'café duty', one of the most important jobs of the volunteers' day, being able to recognise a specific boat as it crossed the harbour mouth was a key skill. Only a few of these small boats are licensed to go to sea – an expensive and bureaucratic business – but there would still be several to choose from as they appeared, a spot at first, from the mouth of the river. Dick Butters's boat, the *Summer Star*, was the easiest to identify, painted bright blue; most of the boats, including Tony's *Nicola Jayne* and Dave Gardner's *Lisa K*, were plain wood. The blue of the *Pania*, and the clear, light turquoise of current island boatman Dave Butters's *Moonraker* would have stood out in the days when most of the boats were plain varnished wood, but they each have a doppelgänger in Looe now.

While the modern boats are handsome and robust, the lightness of, say, the *Nicola Jayne* made her perfect for island crossings. On a calm day, when the fenders – hollow plastic buoys which act as a sort of bumper – were out of the way, I could even as a smallish child reach over the side of the boat and trail my hand through the water, a sensuous ritual of the start of an island holiday, but the sides of the modern boats are too high. With the *Nicola Jayne*'s shallow keel, she could land on the beach with the tide way out: we would run down one or two wooden trolleys, one end of which, on a couple of wheels perhaps two feet high, would butt up against the boat for people to step out on to, and then cover yards of shallows, treacherous with seaweed, with a line of planks, on to the proper dry land of the beach. This allowed Tony to land at almost any tide, so he could bring many more visitors to stay for different lengths of time; now, trips are for two hours only, and only three hours either side of high tide, when there is enough water for the slightly bigger boats. The wooden trolleys did occasionally float out to sea, from where they might or might not be recovered, but their manoeuvrability in comparison to the hugely heavy metal beast of our first winter was a great blessing.

The little wooden boats, vanishing already into nostalgia, were a mainstay of Looe for centuries. In all likelihood, the boats taking the visitors of the Middle Ages, when the island was jostling for position as a top Christian tourist destination, would not have been very different. The island hasn't been so undignified as to jostle for anything for some time now: both the Atkinses and the Wildlife Trust were keen for it to cover its costs as far as possible, but both were equally committed to preserving its wildness, to avoiding commercialisation. It seems odd to think that the opposite was the case so many centuries ago, and in the island's most religious period, with moneymaking and marketing the priorities. When Glastonbury Abbey acquired the island chapel as an outpost in the twelfth century, they wanted a slice of the action they saw at St Michael's Mount, where visiting pilgrims were a key part of the economy with the offerings they brought to the monks who ran the place. Professor Nicholas Orme describes Glastonbury as 'the first English theme park', and St Michael was big business – the most lucrative day of the year was Michaelmas in late September, but there were more St Michael's Days to cash in on in May and October. After Edward the Confessor gave St Michael's Mount to Mont-Saint-Michel, in the endless trading of marginal land between England and France across many centuries, the French seemed to have the St Michael's market completely sewn up – but Glastonbury's marketing department got to work.

Saints were the celebrities of the period, particularly popular in Cornwall, where they were said to have made benign changes to the landscape: opening up holy wells, and routing the giants, who had made more violent changes, littering the place with boulders from their fights and games. The giant Cormoran was responsible for throwing together St Michael's Mount itself. They were a nasty lot, the giants: terrorising the countryside, bullying their wives, stealing and eating children, and their replacement by saints in the lore of the place was a relief, as the place names– St Ives, St Austell, St Just – still reflect.

St George's Island was quickly rebranded as St Michael's, but was going to have a better story than just any old saint. Joseph of Arimathea, a key figure at the Crucifixion, was, perhaps, a merchant and, perhaps, dealt in tin. Babs used to repeat to every group of visitors the story, which evidently reverberated through the old families of Looe through many centuries, of the child Christ playing on the beaches of the island while Joseph negotiated for the tin and copper mined in Cornwall and central to Roman requirements for bronze armour and tools. Bolstered by this local detail, Glastonbury gussied up the Celtic chapel, which probably already existed on the island, first in wood and then in stone, with more decorative doors and windows, and dispatched a Prior Elias and Brother John to 'St Michael de Lammana' – the monks' enclosure.

St Michael rewarded bravery with time off Purgatory, and perhaps this thought comforted them as their vows of obedience kept them steadfast, setting out to sea. In time, and after the loss of a number of monks to obedience, tide and weather, Glastonbury erected another chapel on the mainland facing that on the island, at the same elevation and, as far as the *Time Team* dig of 2008 could discover, in essentially the same layout, to double the chances of pilgrim tourism. When weddings, including ours, take place on the island in the twenty-first century, a similar backup plan – a licensed venue on the mainland – is essential.

It has always been my mother's favourite place, the chapel site, 150 feet above sea level, the peak of the island, away from the earthly grind: a place for poetry, for solitude. The topography doesn't allow you to see, even from there, sea at every angle: perhaps that is a kindness. The maker of one of many TV documentaries asked Attie once if she ever felt claustrophobic, being always in this little 22-acre plot, and she was baffled. 'Claustrophobic? No! I can see how you might feel *agora*phobic . . .' Here, at the top of the island, with nothing between you and the sky, there is a sense of freedom, of exultation. I preferred the safety of the lower reaches of the place, as a child – Jetty Beach, Gull Island – but now, partly because those spaces are often out of bounds, as the Trust protect nesting birds, I spend more time exposed in the higher spaces of air, where the chapel used to be, and find that you can breathe easily there.

Time Team come to the island the year before our plans crystallise, and their finds are fascinating and frustrating in equal measure. Walls indicate the shape and orientation (facing the east) of the chapel: 'a hell of a piece of engineering,' one of the archaeologists marvels. There are small graves cut into the bedrock; a hoard of Roman coins; an oval enclosure around the higher portion of the island, which suggests a prehistoric settlement within. There are anchor stones, with a hole drilled through one end, which have been used since the Iron Age. Amphora fragments from the Aegean, dated around AD 500, were found previously in the garden of Island House, and an ingot of copper and tin, over two thousand years old, was dredged up from the seabed close to the island, although the *Time Team* divers find, disappointingly, no shipwrecks.

If only, you think, someone could do a full dig, months' worth of exploration: three days hardly scratches the surface. I wish I had been there, too, to see the shape of the building exposed, to picture more clearly how the monks must have lived here, how this space must have looked, although watching the excavations on television feels half like a violation.

Documented island history falls largely into three parts: the chapel, the smugglers, and the Atkins sisters. Fascinated by the shadows, I try to research the missing parts: I talk to Mike Dunn, whose mother was a school friend of Attie's and whose book on the history of the island is authoritative; to Barbara Birchwood-Harper, doyenne of the museum in Looe; to local historians and architects; to libraries, records offices; relations and connections of previous occupants. The centuries which span the period between the documented heyday of the chapel and the ripping yarns of smuggling are opaque, the chapel itself sliding into the hillside, and the island into obscurity. A few historians give the island or the chapel a cursory mention: William of Worcester, in his journey from Bristol to St Michael's Mount in 1478, tells us just that 'The island of S. Michael de low lies opposite the town of Low one mile from the mainland.' By the time of the dissolution of the monasteries, the Chantry Commissions reported that 'the service in the chapel hath of late discontinued', and around the same time, John Leland, travel writer of the sixteenth century and the King's Antiquary, makes no mention of a chapel at all in his brief description of the island off the coast of Looe: 'a lowe isle cawle S. Nicholas Isle, not a quarter of a myle far the mayne shore, and conteyneth a Vi or Vii acres of cumpace, and feedeth sheep and conies [rabbits]'. This is the only mention of the island as dedicated to St Nicholas, though as the patron saint of sailors, said to have saved the ship on which he travelled to the Holy Land, rebuking the waves threatening to wreck it in a storm, he would be a pretty useful ally

As an indicator of the island's status as a site of pilgrimage, the loss even of the name of St Michael makes it clear that its heyday is over. It is a side note only in the sixteenth and seventeenth centuries, though the best depiction of it, surrounded by the Spanish Armada, is on a map of 1539, showing a thatched and disproportionately huge chapel. A cannonball allegedly fired from one of those ships used to sit at the door to the café, and formed another set piece of Babs's welcome to visitors, as she invited visiting children to lift its surprising weight when a group of day trippers paused on their way in. By the time of Elizabeth and the Armada, though, the island had become not much more than a navigational aid: soundings are given around it, and anchorage marked out, on a map of 1582, and charts of the seventeenth century – which omit the more famous St Michael's Mount – do show Looe Island. By this time, it was owned by the Mayow(e)s, a prosperous Looe family who owned a good deal of land locally. Richard Carew, in his 1603 *Survey of Cornwall*, reported approvingly of Philip Mayowe that as the island is 'plentifully stored with conies', a visitor 'through the leave and kindness of the Master May, the owner, you may make and take your choice'. A descendant a century or so on was John Mayow, an Oxford scientist who conducted ground-breaking work around combustion and respiration – a pioneer in air. The family was also related to the Mayhews who established Martha's Vineyard in the newly 'discovered' America. The days of influential private owners had begun.

As for the chapel, it vanished, from public consciousness and eventually of course from physical being. When Thomas Bond, a Looe expert, comes to write about the island in 1823, it has largely disintegrated; he mentions 'the remains of some building, which goes by the name of the Chapel'. The three houses on the island, all dated somewhere around the nineteenth century but at least some evidently replacing older buildings on the same site, are constructed largely of stone. Building on the island is brutally difficult, and a large quantity of good stone in a derelict building would surely be irresistible to the pragmatic subsistence farmers of later periods. Excavations of the chapel site make it clear that it was plundered extensively: they throw up sherds of pottery from the thirteenth century, from the sixteenth; rubbish of all sorts from the nineteenth; evidence of an exhumation from the eighteenth. All point towards centuries of disturbance, for practical or scientific or superstitious reasons.

By the time of Ward, Lock and Co.'s Guide of 1948, the chapel has disappeared. All that is visible now are a couple of carved stones of dubious antiquity. The quiet remains of stone walls, mortared floors, carved burial chambers and old bones lie hidden again under the springy turf and loamy soil: anonymous hands have healed the hill's gashes.

The reality of winter accessibility to our new home made us thoughtful, exactly as the trial was intended to, but we were cautiously prepared to be hermits. Apart from that one foray back to the mainland, we stayed on the island, cold but contented, and planned. We ventured timidly to our new house every day, calling out softly to the startled ghosts as we opened the door. The notion of straying beyond the edge of the hall had been so forbidden for so many years that I felt guilty every time I stepped in, and the cold, the dark and the dust combined to dampen the spirits. There was no working electricity in the house, and December daylight doesn't illuminate much. Although there were many spiders ('I wish you wouldn't do that,' Patrick sighed, as I screamed and dropped the tape measure), I missed the dogs, and their steady movement, and the smell of the house when the sisters were here, a comfortable mix of baking, whisky and dog.

We measured and planned. We wondered whether to repurpose the downstairs rooms, according to a vision Sheila suggested, so that the kitchen would be in the huge, windowed sitting room, and the sitting room in the smaller, snugger kitchen, the old scullery a nice little office, or 'library', or 'music room'. But then where, Patrick asked anxiously, would we hang our salamis? Practicality, including considerations of flooring (magnificent slate in the kitchen, rat-eaten boards in the sitting room), encouraged us to keep the rooms as they were. Or at least, as they were designed to be: there was no sink in the kitchen, no water to the house, and the bathroom hadn't been used for years.

We researched composting toilets: digging a septic tank into the rocky ground was an off-putting thought, and we couldn't continue to flush sewage into the sea, as the 'helpers' loo' always used to. The key feature of composting loos seems to be that they are astonishingly ugly; we toyed with the idea of constructing an imposing Victorian-style cabinet to add some gravitas. Beautiful Jason emailed to warn us that he found them problematic because his balls knocked awkwardly on the separation box at the front, but green living trumped other considerations, and we put an order in.

As the years pass, I regret vetoing Patrick's enthusiastic suggestion that we should build our own. The system we buy has different levels, trays and levers, designed to keep liquid waste separate and allow the 'humanure' to dry out, but these quickly jam and overflow. The whirligig on the roof which provides ventilation is continually seizing; a product we were recommended to use to assist composting introduces catastrophic flies. Whenever the user count is higher than the two of us, a heady smell of ammonia accompanies any change in temperature (such as day to evening), and open chemical warfare cannot banish the infestation. The quarterly task of emptying the box is a choking process of scoops and buckets, trips with a wheelbarrow to the designated bin next to the compost heap, grateful washing up with the hose which in the summer spouts warm water from the black tanks. Eventually, we substitute a simpler 'poo bin' system based on a dustbin and a hose, and crowbar out the old container, rusted into the cupboard in Patrick's fragrant office just under the bathroom, settling it under the tamarisk trees until we think of a new use for it, or borrow the muscle to get it taken to the tip.

We marvel, now that summers always bring a water shortage, at the amount of clean water wasted on flushing lavatories, and at two years or so the contents of our loo metamorphose into scentless, friable compost. We are acutely conscious of the various kinds of waste we produce, and recycling of some sort is the aim wherever possible. In the seventies, when 'environment' was not yet a watchword, the boatman would chuck our black bags of rubbish overboard, weighted down with a stone; sewage from the lavatories poured raw into the sea near the jetty. Large items went 'over cliff', as Daphne du Maurier (whom Ernie, a Polruan boy, used to row about in the river from Fowey) described the rubbish disposal of her time, just a few miles round the coast. Now, we seem to be taking stuff off the island – rubbish, recycling, empty gas bottles – as much as we're bringing supplies on. Appropriate food scraps are composted here; paper and cardboard are burned and the ashes added to the compost heap. Anything else recyclable goes to the relevant bins at the tip near Liskeard, and 'landfill', as Jon warningly labels that bin in his kitchen, is kept to a minimum.

Although Patrick's enthusiasm for the project was unaffected, he started to struggle as the cold, inactive weeks of that first winter stay passed; he wouldn't of course admit to the muscle pain which was clearly plaguing him, symptom of a genetic condition he always tried to ignore. He worked grimly away in the window alcove of the old barn, where the helpers' parties used to be held around a big table with window seats on three sides; where we made boxes for daffodils by post on rainy March days; where the registrars who married us stood, after the table had gone, and where now there are handsome French windows leading outside. Between the generator's morning and afternoon stints, he relied on his laptop battery, and on a monstrously heavy battery pack and 'uninterruptable power supply' which we lugged with us.

He made less fuss than I about the unremitting cold, and his researches into island living were much more valuable than my virtual model of where the furniture might go. After four weeks, we were pretty clear about the way forwards: how to access water and electricity; how to arrange plumbing and drainage; what to do about heat and the internet, essential for us to work here. We managed a critical meeting with Jon's boss Callum, along with the Trust's lawyer and a land agent, and a detailed schedule of works was agreed, to be begun in March, which would give us the longest possible run at the renovation before winter claimed the sea again.

We had one bright day towards the end of our stay, and I walked round the far side of the island marvelling at the clear paths and open spaces, thanks to the grazing sheep and all Jon's work. I felt suddenly very happy. I explored what would be our plot of land, which was sizeable, and although it was behind the house, it sloped upwards, so that if we were to build a shed up there, as an extra room, it could still have beautiful views. I pictured pigs rooting up the ground, and dreamed of planting, having cleared the half-acre thicket of bramble and ivy: perennials in the flower beds, flowering shrubs, vegetables. We had an orchard already – an old apple orchard – and a miniature wild-flower meadow, a patch of yellow rattle, bacon-and-egg plant, speedwell and ox-eye daisies, which Jon had planted next to the fruit trees.

We left before Christmas, but we met Gus and Sheila in Island House first to decorate their Christmas tree, too tall for their cottage, which they put in here to cheer the place every year. In woolly hats and gloves, we hung ornaments, ate mince pies and attempted a carol: a moment of festivity before our stormy embarkation for a snow-bound Christmas with my mother in the Yorkshire Dales. She suspected this might be her last Christmas in the stone house high on a hill with spectacular views across the dale, and we wanted to be with her to celebrate it. A rare condition which clamps her eyelids closed for minutes at a time meant that her driving days were numbered, so 25 years in her perfect house were about to come to an end, just as we prepared to move into ours. Having survived our winter trial, this departure marked our final absence from our new home.

Just over two months later, on the last, coldest day of February, there is enough of a break in the wild weather of winter for us to cross from the mainland, with our tins of soup and curry, bags of compost, two appalled cats in their boxes. We walk up from the beach, the shingle path crunching under our feet, and as we crest the hill, the house appears, suddenly, ahead of us, tired white walls glinting in the failing light. We open the rattling front door with what we hope is a suitable mixture of tact and confidence, and move in by torchlight.

It has been empty now for six years, and it is full of ghosts. The tall man the dressmaker saw, with his long fingers and a blue light behind him; the sisters in their flowered nylon, Attie's eyes remorselessly magnified behind her glasses; my childhood self, waiting at the doorstep for a batch of scones. Every wall is patterned with black mould, in lacy fronds or lumpy stripes; every window in the house is broken.

We pile bedding, blankets, coats on to the bed and the cats climb in with us, mourning their lost comforts. We listen to the wails of wind and the menace of waves through the broken glass, and breathe in the spores and the damp, clinging together, our family, in the faint warmth of the bed.

We are entirely happy.

Chapter 6

Previous Owners

―――――

benign ghosts dissolved
in sunshine: monks, smugglers, farmers, coastguards

Chris Considine, *Island Wedding*

Island House is not a very old house, but it has seen many changes in its time. The Trelawny family, powerful Cornish landowners, owned the island for centuries; by the late nineteenth century, they had had tenant farmers here for many decades, and when we clear patches of bramble now, we often find wonderful, fertile cultivated soil for which we have them to thank. However good the farmers might have been, though, there was always the threat of undesirables using the island, its hidden shores and inlets, for their own ends. In the New Year of 1876, the Trelawnys resolved to formalise its management, and our house was conceived.

Eighty years earlier, local legend whispered that 'Black Joan' Finn had murdered a black man on the island, though no one seems sure exactly who he was – a trader, a slave, a lover? *A Book of Cornwall*, written by chronicler of Cornish tales and histories Sabine Baring-Gould, at the turn of the twentieth century, tells us that when they came to the island, the Finns 'were joined by a negro, and by their united efforts honeycombed the ground under their hovel and the large barn adjoining for the accommodation of smuggled goods . . . One day the black man vanished, and it was never known what had become of him, whether he had left or been murdered by Fyn and his sister. There were naturally no witnesses; nothing could be proved against them.'

The Finns, 'as wild as their companion seabirds', came to the island with their father Thomas, previously exiled for seven years to the bare Mewstone – more a rock than an island – off the shore of Plymouth, for being 'a nuisance to his neighbours'. There were no neighbours now: 'There is only one house on the island,' an anonymous visitor tells us in 1793, 'which is inhabited by an old man and his family, consisting of 8 including some grand children . . . We came in the middle of harvest and saw them taking in their corn . . . the old man said he kept a horse and two cows and told me he thought there were about 22 acres of culpable land in the island . . .' For Thomas Finn, the Mewstone Man, this subsistence farming sounds luxurious, idyllic, quite apart from his fabled ill-gotten riches. If the fables are to be believed, these must have been considerable.

'Free trade' was thriving in the eighteenth and nineteenth

centuries, and the island was an invaluable asset. Not only was it possible to land goods out of sight of the mainland, but there are endless rumours, including Baring-Gould's, of superb hiding places which were known only to the Finns – and after them, the Hoopers – and not even to the seagoing smugglers. Mike Dunn relates the first-hand account of 'an old Cawsand smuggler' who explains: 'They had a cave somewhere, but no one ever found it; and they took jolly good care no one should see them put the tubs into it – they always sent the chaps inside the house while that was going on.' If even their smuggling colleagues had no idea where the caves were, the Customs men had no chance of finding them: 'the coastguard came off to the island, almost before Hamram [Hooper] had properly cleared up his place after stowing away the tubs . . . and they searched and dug all over the island for days, but they found nothing. The tubs – there were three hundred of 'em – lay in the caves on Looe island for three months.'

Although there are caves, with authentic bats, to the west of the island, around High Cove, where I have swum with my family and walked, at low tide, with my brother, and lingered with my teenage boyfriend, they are not deep: unless there are further caves we cannot penetrate, they would be inadequate hiding places. The intermediary who related the smuggler's tale assures us that the Hoopers' caves have in fact been found, but the only discovery of them at the edge of living memory was by some casual picnickers. Babs used to tell the story of how these visitors happened to fall through the floor of the big barn which became Jetty Cottage, but there is no evidence that the space there is very extensive. More thrillingly, a *Cornish Times* article in 1900 presented as fact the 'discovery' that 'At a distance of about 18ft below the surface, St George's Island was nothing but an extensive ramification of caves.' These appear to date back to 800 BC; some of them are brick-built, and may originally have been above ground: more detail to appear in the next issue! But the next issue of the paper was silent on the subject.

The relationships between smugglers, their allies and their enemies were complex. The Finns and the Hoopers – many of the stories of island smuggling conflate the two families and they seem to have been inter-related – evidently didn't trust the seafarers who brought the goods from France. Their allies on the mainland were necessary in providing information on the movements of Customs officials, but were double agents who gave information to whoever paid. The best known of those allies was a local farmer who would signal 'clear' to the island by riding his white horse home, west along Hannafore. If the Customs men were poised to swoop, then the farmer would walk, and lead his horse: on those days, he could say, his horse seemed lame. The Finns used lights when they needed to signal. Babs and Attie's great-nephew, Colin, told us that this was the story of the 'secret room', the space above a bay window in the house with no access, but little windows at either end: a light would be placed there to alert the crew of the relevant boats to danger, or to an auspicious night for activity. Most brutal of the double-crosses was a Finn turning Queen's evidence on Hooper at Portwrinkle Bay. The local beach and inn are both now known as Finnygook: Finn's ghost is tied there by guilt.

The authorities were incensed by the slipperiness of the island smugglers, and set up one of their men on the island itself to try and put a stop to their lawlessness. Babs and Attie understood that the Customs house which was built on the island was Island House, its deceptively imposing exterior designed to intimidate. In fact it was first, according to a newspaper, 'a Coastguard station . . . built of wood and 12 feet square, with an iron pipe through the roof for a chimney, similar to a caravan' – evidently, the authorities were desperate to get something in place quickly. It's likely that this was succeeded by the little cottage at the edge of the wood now, romantically, known as Smugglers Cottage. In the twentieth century, this was the gardener's cottage for more than one owner of the island, then a holiday let, where we stayed as children. Although the sycamore had insinuated itself right up to the back of the house, making the bedrooms there gloomy and greenish and off-putting to a child, the rooms at the front were bright and the garden a sun-trap. The cottage fell into disrepair as the sisters aged, housing helpers with only marginally more comfort than the huts by Island House, the smaller bedroom uninhabitable, with spectacular patterned growths of different moulds. It was rescued by Gus and Sheila, who lived there for 16 years and made it warm and comfortable again, the sycamore pushed back, the garden full of figs and flowers.

Even the constant presence of an official on the island made little difference to the smuggling activities: 'Partly,' says Sabine Baring-Gould, 'through Black Joan's fascinations, mainly through the liberal flow of drink at the hut of the Fyns, and the tedium of the long evenings in solitude.' Black Joan was evidently not above using her feminine wiles: there's a story of her running to the Customs man on the island, wailing that her boat had pulled away from its moorings and was drifting out to sea. He kindly set off in his own boat to retrieve it, leaving the other side of the island free for a landing of contraband.

More respectable tenant farmers replaced the smugglers, in the 'small dwelling-house and an out-house, which are situated in the lowest part of the island and appear antient buildings', as described by Looe's foremost tour guide of the early nineteenth century, Thomas Bond. The Vagues, whose descendants now live in one of the prettiest houses in Looe, had half a dozen children born here in the 1850s, the family as fertile as the loamy land. We bless them as we plant our vegetables behind the house in the deep earth, carefully cultivated by centuries of seaweed and muck.

Which house, we wonder, is the one where Baring-Gould reported in 1913, 'In Looe Island, off East and West Looe, is still, or was a few years ago, a skull preserved in a cupboard in the sitting-room, behind glass'? He offers no other information, but was writing about 'screaming skulls', the skulls which have been preserved as objects of veneration, or perhaps as trophies, and whose removal from a house causes uproar and upheaval within it until they are returned. Whose skull was it; why did it scream; and where is it now?

Perhaps it was Black Joan's (or Jochabed's) black companion? Was he the 'remarkably large human skeleton' Bond reported as being found buried at the top of the island? Or – and? – the ghost the dressmaker saw, staying overnight on the island in 1850: a tall man with long fingers, emerging in a blue light from one wall, moving slowly across the room to disappear through the opposite one. It is overwhelmingly tempting to link the long-fingered ghost, the long-thighed skeleton at the chapel site, the screaming skull and the murdered black man, to weave together stories from the fragments of memory, imagination, history and myth. Babs was told that the slope to the east of the chapel site concealed dozens of bodies of drowned monks, and *Time Team* concluded, unofficially, something similar. Baring-Gould tells us soberly that 'Actually there is a layer of human remains about two feet below the surface of the turf, exposed on the east side of the island, where wind and spray are gnawing away the cliff, and any number of teeth and bones may be picked out. Whether these are the remains of an early Christian monastic cemetery, or of shipwrecked sailors buried on the cliffs, cannot be told, as no investigation has been made to discover the approximate period to which this layer of dead men's bones belongs.'

I peer every winter at the freshly scraped cliffs, where the sea has torn at the soft sides of the island, revealing neat, geography-lesson layers of earth and stones, half hoping and half fearing to see the smooth curve of a skull, the extrusion of bone.

Lady Harriet Trelawny wished, perhaps, to banish fables of treasure in caves and skulls in cabinets; of thwarted public servants and spectacular thefts; to reclaim the island from fecund farmers. She was a lady of determination and resourcefulness, and a committed diarist; it seems quite just that her diaries are among the few records to survive the twentieth-century ravages – war, fire – which destroyed so many Trelawny papers. She resolved that the island should become respectable.

By the end of January 1876, the weather had calmed sufficiently for the Trelawnys to travel to the island which was really a throwaway part of their property portfolio, and on the 27th, they embarked on a small boat for the mile-long journey. How would they have agreed on the most appropriate site for the house? The island must have seemed smaller then; it was treeless for centuries, and the tree-planting of the mid nineteenth century would not yet have dominated; the 22 acres would have been seen more clearly as a large, undulating field. The Trelawnys would have wanted a flattish site, sheltered by the hill from the worst of the weather from the west. They would have wanted it near to the spring, and close to a spot where a boat could land. The location must have become less of a choice, less of a question: the ghosts and ruins of former buildings would have presented themselves persuasively. The ramshackle farm of the disreputable Finns and fertile Vagues replaced in its time another farmhouse, not far away. There was by 1876 a solid, newish barn in this flat, sheltered spot, and a long granite wall which the Trelawnys shored up and adorned with battlements. Whether that was part of an older building, or a fancy windbreak, is not clear.

That wall runs still from the house to the barn which is now Jetty Cottage, with the ruins of Babs's great greenhouse in between, and hydrangeas and honeysuckle thriving at the front. There is a brick-topped archway in the wall forming the gateway to our house, and the wind whips through the tunnel formed there, flings dustbins about, burns the herbs in pots by our door, tears the lid off the rainwater butt.

The house is built solidly, but without frills. It is imposing, but smaller than it looks: a Tardis in reverse. It was built to last, to impress without bragging, to accommodate without luxury. It was good enough for a servant, a caretaker whose title would, the Trelawnys decided, be Keeper of the Island. It was carefully designed, perhaps by the local architect of choice, Henry Rice, whose handsome buildings adorn the locality. To look at, it is more substantial than the two up, two down which is all the useful space it actually offers, a solid two storeys of gables, bay windows and a chaos of roof heights which look like afterthoughts. They are not, Rice's successors assure us; the building has been carefully planned. The four-roomed accommodation forms the bar of a T shape, with the foot accommodating a handsome, unnecessarily roomy staircase with a pyramid for a roof. Everything about it is considered, deliberate. Under Lady Trelawny's aegis, how could it have been otherwise?

The kitchen, hall and scullery are floored with huge flagstones set directly on to the earth: splendid, but usually damp. The rest of the house is boarded in pine, and the sitting-room walls are panelled against the damp which rises inexorably from the earth beneath; at least it is a sunny room, south-facing, and the walls are feet thick. Panoramic sea views are an inevitability, not an ingenious gift from the architect: did they move Messrs Nicholas, Walters and Williams, glancing at the weather before they left the house to undertake their Keeping? Did these servants of the Trelawnys have any choice about coming to the island; did they long for the relative comforts of the mainland, or revel in the autonomy of their little kingdom here?

Like our mainland cottage, Island House was built with functionality in mind and to house workers, but the passage of time has given such houses, to today's sentimental middle classes, the allure of history. Within twelve months of living here, I appreciate for the first time our grandparents' longing for the new, the modern, which left so many 'period properties' with an ugly mid-twentieth-century facelift, their fireplaces and cornicing and flagstone floors ripped out and smoothed over. I come to understand the wonder of plastic, of central heating and mains services, of fitted bathrooms and kitchens and carpets.

*

The one modern convenience that we can't survive without on the island is the internet. As we are neither retired, like Gus and Sheila, nor essentially working the land, like Jon and Claire, we need to earn a living. Justin, Patrick's old friend, business partner and the inventor of the software they're taking to market, is buoyed up by the sale of his last business, and we are cushioned by the sale of our house: the two of them have enjoyed a leisurely few months of designing logos, signing documents and ordering branded mugs, and there is no great sense of urgency, but without internet, we won't be able to survive here long-term.

There is 3G mobile coverage, which works pretty well for us, but as soon as a mast goes down for maintenance on the mainland or the signal drops out in bad weather, we're in trouble. Patrick's technical brain relishes the challenge: he fine-tunes the connectivity via 'directional antennae', and spends a frightening chunk of time on the flat roof of the 1940s extension to the house. The ground floor used to be the boiler room, with a section hived off as the helpers' loo, and will now be Patrick's office at ground level with the vaguely art deco bathroom above. He is busy and cheerful among the wires of communications, and in exploring and redesigning the wiring of the house, which will be our first project. He brings a technical and practical expertise to the renovation and glories, stimulated and fulfilled, in solving problem after problem of island life.

As he starts to take more potential customers through the

details of the product online, in hour-long screen-sharing calls, he realises that a backup system is essential, and a satellite dish moves incongruously into the garden, tucked into a corner by an escallonia hedge and facing out to sea. The telephone is not a comfortable instrument for someone with his hearing problems – he has been profoundly deaf since birth, though years of speech therapy and ever-improving hearing aids mitigate this considerably. Nor do sales seem a natural fit for someone with his natural impatience, but he turns out to his own surprise to be highly successful. By the end of our first year on the island, the business has secured a couple of good-sized clients and a part-time salesman with the tenacity and charm which, it transpires, are needed for cold calling.

I volunteer for this in the first instance, eager to help. My first job, as a callow graduate with no idea about how to earn money, picking up whatever I could get from the *Evening Standard* jobs page, was cold calling. I turned up on a raw morning in Leytonstone, an eastern extremity of London, to discover that we were selling lint removers door to door. I lasted half a day at that. I still have to nerve myself to pick up the phone to shops, tradesmen, anyone I don't know, and often people I do.

But, I reason to myself, to Patrick, surely you have a kind of script, you can hide behind that, how hard can it be? That is Patrick's motto, which is why he has started this embryonic business on an island and in the depths of a catastrophic recession; and I think I should man up.

I have spent an afternoon, in preparation, with an old friend of Patrick's who's a whiz at sales. She's made a few calls for them, but hasn't time to do more: she does her best to furnish me with approaches and tips so I now feel ready to tackle the magazine publishers of the world.

'Oh hallo, I'm calling on behalf of some friends who've recently set up a business, and we just wanted to get an idea of whether you might be interested in their software. So it's basically a CRM system—'

'What's CRM?'

This is absolutely not part of my script. That's supposed to mean something to them! How on earth am I supposed to know?

'So basically, the software manages the life cycle of a magazine and all the placing of adverts and your records—'

'What do you mean, the life cycle?'

No idea.

'So – it manages the whole process from, you know, start to finish, so it makes it all a lot slicker and—'

'We're happy with what we've got, thank you.'

I make four calls. None of the people I speak to stick to the script, and I am in tears of frustration and wounded pride as I suggest to Patrick and Justin that actually, what with the house and the garden, I might just have too much on my hands to devote myself to sales.

*

We are another, tiny chapter in the story of how it's possible to live, financially speaking, on the island, as we coincide with the change in technology which allows millions of people, suddenly, to do most of their work from home; with the surge in self-employment; with the great shift in almost all businesses, certainly all our clients', from paper to screen.

Babs and Attie, in the 1960s, were part of the great social shift of the twentieth century. They were 'pioneers': independent single women whose financial wherewithal was largely self-created, with a freedom their mother ('the Lady', as she was known) wouldn't have dreamed of. A generation earlier, two sisters of their age without great wealth or status to buoy them could surely never have found the cash or the confidence to buy the island, or the help they needed to succeed there. Earlier occupants of the island were self-sufficient farmers, or wealthy retirees with staff, and the turn of the previous century heralded the change from one to another.

The building of Island House, shortly before the dawn of the twentieth century, saw a new era for the island, as private, wealthy, often eccentric owners began to make their mark. For centuries, since the waning of its popularity as a place of religious pilgrimage, it had been – along with many properties which are now deeply treasured – a throwaway outpost of a great family's lands, looked after by tenants and servants. The Trelawnys, the greatest of Cornish families, were the last such feudal owners. It was a particularly charming whim of Babs's to leave the family an outcrop of the island – our Gull Island – and a perfect expression of gratitude for Sir John's patient help in planning for the island's future life after her own death. His son, also Sir John, who is now the unassuming head of the family, and perhaps not far from my age, visited us a couple of times and surveyed his windswept scrap of land with proper appreciation.

Even before the end of the Trelawnys' tenure, with the handsome house in place, the island was being let to monied romantics with gardeners, rather than the tenant farmers of previous centuries. Due to its location, the island has, between and within these tenancies, had the occasional brush with the military, from being surrounded by the Armada in the sixteenth century to being bombed in the Second World War. Around the time of the Napoleonic wars, the setting for Arthur Quiller-Couch's 'The Looe Die-Hards', a story celebrating the extraordinary ability to survive of the entire East and West Looe Volunteer Artillery, Looe sent 21 ships (more than anywhere else except London) to a critical battle at sea. It was the exceptional performance of the battleship *St George* which, Attie was given to understand, caused the island's name finally to change from St Michael's to St George's. In 1894, the island itself became a defender of the realm: *Cassell's Gazetteer* tells us that 'the island [has] been converted into a coastguard station. A battery with three guns now defends the harbour.' Attie agreed that 'there is an old gun emplacement on the island facing due south', though I have never found it. The crater left by the landmine dropped by a German plane is still very visible, though, near the top of the island where the woods fade to grassland, and a fascination to small boys who visit us. Older inhabitants of Looe are less entranced: they remember the noise, the smoke, the windows and greenhouses smashing along Hannafore. The *Cornish Times* described the incident with gleeful facetiousness, with the headline 'HMS *St George*. Nazi Airman's Direct Hit Off Looe – Another "Success" for the Luftwaffe': popular belief was that a German airman mistook the island for a ship.

It was shortly after the First World War that the Trelawnys gave up St George's Island and it passed into private hands. The die was cast, really, by the time the house was built. The Keepers – caretakers – of the Island were there briefly, but then a couple of long-term private tenants came in: the Trelawnys were starting to relinquish responsibility. Ezra Neale (and sub-tenants) was there in the 1880s, a potato merchant with a genius for becoming embroiled in low-level crime: as a victim of fraud; charged with drunkenness; threatened with death for employing the Irish; and, on the island, furiously dismissing his caretaker ('a thief, a rogue and a poacher,' he roared) for being in possession of a gun with which he dared to shoot island rabbits. The days of the generous Master Mayow, his conies free for all, were long gone.

The rabbits and rats of the island have been a vexed question over the centuries. The *West Briton* reported that 'A strange piece of folklore', in connection with the Finns, 'claims the siblings . . . ate every rat and rabbit on the island.' That doesn't seem so strange, for impoverished occupants to eat everything edible in a finite space, though at other times those edibles have been more of a nuisance. Wilkie Collins talks in *Rambles Beyond Railways* of the island rats, thought to have come ashore from shipwrecks, decimating the crops and cultivated land until the whole of Looe was invited for a days'-long mammoth rat hunt. At the end of each day, the rats were '*smothered in onions*; the corpses were then decently laid out on clean china dishes, and straightway eaten with vindictive relish by the people of Looe' (the current wardens make and sell a 'Vindictive Relish' in the visitor centre), and hence the rats were annihilated in the middle of the nineteenth century.

Rabbits were similarly wiped out in the middle of the twentieth, with shooting parties to remove them as they stuffed themselves on early flowers and bulbs. By the twenty-first century, rats were back with a vengeance, but the Wildlife Trust managed a successful cull when they took over the island. When I was younger, the rats were absolutely rife. Babs's dogs, and cats, hunted them and killed a few, but they were everywhere: a whole colony under the Chalet where we used to stay, noisy through the nights. My friend Ingela didn't believe it when she came for a holiday with me, until she put a piece of cheese a few feet away from the front door to test my tales, and watched aghast as a rat pounced within seconds.

The last tenant before the Trelawnys finally sold the island, and the subsequent owners until Babs and Attie bought it in the sixties, were all men (of course) of means. Henry St John Dix, who leased the island for 21 years, was a successful engineer, master of reservoirs and railways, bridges and sewers: bankruptcy forced him to leave after nine. Paul Corder, fellow of the Royal Academy of Music, bought the island in 1921, and visited often with his sister Dorothea and their musical friends. 'Myra Hess played here,' Attie used to tell us, in the big room in Jetty Cottage. 'This used to be a music room.' It was always an odd thought, that other world of culture and furs and scent, colliding with the uncompromising stone of the barn, the violent wind from the south-east. 'I do remember "Aunty" Dolly when I was a child in the 1950s,' the Corders' distant cousin Denis Malsher writes to me. 'She was living in Surrey in her latter years, and I remember her house was furnished with fine clocks and furniture.' The Island House must have been too, elegant at last. An advertisement for the island in the early twentieth century mentions a 'glass corridor', which seems to have linked Island House and Jetty Cottage, where Babs's greenhouse stood later: that sounds rather glamorous, orangery-like, and would have taken guests straight to the 'annexe' and music room. I like to picture this episode of gracious living, the mould and the woodlice kept at bay by servants and the romance of candlelight.

After Paul died, Dolly sold the island: again, it was used as a holiday home rather than a main residence, the house unfurnished as far as Gavin Kingerlee, whose grandfather Charles became the new owner of the island in 1943, remembers. Charles Kingerlee, who lived a convenient mile from the island in a handsome house he built by the quay in West Looe, was evidently a character – a local benefactor who took all the local children to the pantomime every year, then to tea, and sent them home with an orange each. He was clearly a vivid figure in Looe. Sharking became (and still is) enormously popular there in the twentieth century, and Charles was one of the first to catch a shark locally: later, the Kingerlees went sharking with Ernie, whose son Philip is now one of the primary shark fishermen in Looe, running chartered boat trips throughout the summer, fishing for cod, mackerel or sole during the winter from the scarlet *Typhoon*.

Gavin remembers smaller-scale fishing: prawning for island lunches: 'I loved the rock pools,' he tells us, when we meet him in his house on Hannafore with its spectacular island views, 'especially with a prawn in them.' Prawns, along with the pilchards which Looe used to land by the tonne, are hard to find now. The other pursuit he remembers vividly is the rabbit shoots which his father and grandfather organised in the woods – Mr Kingerlee wished, as did some of his successors, to run the island as a market garden, producing early daffodils. The woods were already well established by this point, though for the vast majority of its history, the island had been treeless. A newspaper cutting of 1926 tells us that 'Seventy years ago . . . there was only one tree on the island. About 60 years ago . . . a great many bundles of young fir trees were planted.' Early photographs of the island show a very neat, small oblong of trees above Smugglers Cottage: now, the trees straggle right down to the shore.

The island continued to grow, after the Kingerlees' time, as a producer of bulbs and spring flowers, with full-time workers both living on and (presumably seasonally) commuting to the island to manage this. Mr Kenward, retired managing director of the Connaught Rooms in London, has, I think, the distinction of being the first owner of the island – certainly for hundreds of years – to live there full-time. His tenure was short: he left after three years, 'giving it up because of his age,' the *Cornish Guardian* reported, 'he is 69.' He was a brave man to take it on at 66, perhaps hoping for more years of youthful vigour. The same newspaper article reported that he was the man to install electricity here, a huge step for the island, which his successor took forwards with gusto.

Major General Rawlins made a terrific impact on both the island and those who knew him. Born in the West Country – and in a particularly beautiful spot, the Elizabethan manor Siston Court, not far from Bristol – it seems fitting that he ended up on the island, after a particularly glittering army career. Commissioned in 1916, at 19, he had by the end of the First World War been awarded the Military Cross – twice – and been wounded in action. As a Royal Artillery commander, he was a key figure in many of the critical operations of the

Second World War, including the Normandy landings; he was known for leading from the front and picked up a DSO and, later, a CBE. His first wife died in childbirth, and one of his two sons was killed in the Second World War: he deserved his island retirement.

He was clear from the start, though, that the island would have to pay its way to supplement the war pension which was otherwise his only income. He found a tremendous ally in Theo Matthews, who moved into Smugglers Cottage as his gardener, along with his family. Theo's son Colin was immortalised by the second Mrs Rawlins, who worked as an illustrator under the name Joyce Bruce: he appears on the cover of children's book *Richard and the Golden Horseshoe*. His was surely an idyllic childhood in the summers, though lodging ashore in the winters to attend school – as Babs did in the following decades – must have been endlessly frustrating: the island, his family, the charismatic general, a stone's throw away but unreachable.

Theo was a 'cliff worker', an expert in growing in frost-free conditions to produce vegetables for sale earlier than they would be available elsewhere. Daffodils were a major crop, as they still were when the Atkinses first arrived on the island and sold to Covent Garden, and much prized by the markets to which they were sent. The general facilitated Theo's transformation of the island into a productive market garden with his development of the electrical installation the Kenwards had begun, building a room near the beach to house his generators and their great square glass batteries, and, in the days before radio, devising an ingenious system of signals to communicate with the mainland. Patrick would have loved him.

He died at 58, on the train to London, after only five years on the island. The only flowers at his funeral were island daffodils.

After his death, his wife tried, as the Kingerlee family had before, to sell the island to Looe District Council. In her letter to them, she explained that she 'believed the island should belong to Looe, whose inhabitants seemed very attached to it. I dread the idea of selling it to someone who might commercialise it and ruin its beauty,' she added. She offered it to them for what sounds like a pretty reasonable £9,000, open to negotiation – the Kingerlee family, prompted by similar sentiments, had offered it for £6,000 some years earlier. 'Paradise though it is,' the council commented, 'we cannot afford it.'

What a shame. Access to the island has been a vexed question in recent decades: older residents of Looe fondly remember boating out there to picnic in the summer, but by the time of the Whitehouses, the Atkinses' predecessors, who had made their money in greenhouses, landing was strictly discouraged. There was considerable disgruntlement when locals began to be 'ordered off' the island: sources disagree on whether this was before or after the island changed hands, but Attie reported that 'after the war Major General Rawlins, who owned the island then, would let local people picnic on the main beach. The tale we were told was that someone had come up and damaged his greenhouse, so he withdrew the facility and to stop "uninvited guests" brought out a shotgun to shoot over the heads of would-be intruders.'

The most vexed question is around the inflammatory subject of boundaries, which seems slightly extraordinary for an island. There is a general sense that anyone should be permitted to land at least on the beach, partly on the grounds that the Crown owns the land between high and low water, country-wide. In the case of the island, though, the story goes that the Prince of Wales, later to be Edward VII, lost the foreshore rights to the owner of the island in a night of gambling. There is endless dispute about the truth of this, but Attie reported that Mr Whitehouse 'had had the facts verified legally and had paid a large sum of money to have the rights incorporated in the deeds'. Even now, kayakers are strongly discouraged from landing on the beach or rocks around the island: under the Wildlife Trust's aegis, this is in the interests of protecting the nesting birds and seals.

In fact, rights to the foreshore are something of a mixed blessing. At the point in the 1920s where a whale became stranded, and died, on the island, it was considered to be the Duchy of Cornwall's problem to shift it. The Atkinses had a picture of eight men, arms stretched out between them, showing the length of it: it was a big beast, which resisted removal by fire and by butchery, finally succumbing to dynamite and showering fragments of rotten whale meat over the locality.

The *Cornish Guardian* reported approvingly when the

sisters were heard to be considering opening the island for a licence fee to visitors brought by an approved boatman. 'The days when Looe Urban Council could have acquired the island as a public open space . . . are gone. Thus the new idea . . . would seem to be the next best thing.' The sisters, already middle-aged when they arrived, and without independent means, local contacts or – whisper it – men, needed all the approval they could get. And, tickled, charmed by Attie, Looe raised an eyebrow, and then looked after them, those unexpected custodians of the island.

They were also bound to need physical help to manage the 22 acres – maintaining paths among the strangle of bramble and ivy; preparing ground to plant and grow and harvest the fruit and vegetables which could sustain them for months; tending to the visitors who brought in hard cash; heaving fuel and shopping and all kinds of supplies on and off boats. They couldn't have found this for free earlier in the century, in a more rigid world of staff and employers; and with their moderate means and limited, if indomitable, energy, they couldn't have employed the full-time help they needed, or managed, physically, without it. They were of their time, though: in the sixties and seventies, volunteering became fashionable, and their shifting cohort of helpers made the physical work possible.

A succession of boatmen got them installed, brought the help and the income from tourists, and kept them supplied through summer and winter for forty years, through illness and old age.

They were brave, determined, practical and charming, the sisters; they paid generously where they needed to, and bought from their volunteers, who gained as much as they gave, love and loyalty and a desire to contribute to the well-being of both the island and its owners.

Living alone on the island from September to April, Babs and Attie were here between them for almost forty winters, and relied increasingly on the faithful Tony for the latter thirty. Although local girl Ruth, the daughter of a market gardener, kept her company in the earliest months, for the next 11 winters, Attie was almost completely alone – before mobile phones, before internet connectivity, limited to an occasional radio telephone call with Babs, or a wave to her at Hannafore, and perhaps a fortnightly boat. Hour after hour and day after day of solitude, of wind-blown trudges to the generator shed, of cold and damp and limited supplies or occupation, lonely toothaches or colds or falls, unleavened moments of depression or despair.

Fifty years after Attie's solitary winters, I spend winter days and nights on the island by myself, when Patrick is away seeing clients, in Attie's house. There is an atmosphere to being alone here, not unease or anxiety but a sort of denseness to the air, a solidity in the silence. Without something alive inside the house to ground you – my cats, Attie's dog – I think you might wheel howling into the night, unable to resist the despair of the wind and the gulls.

Chapter 7

Renovation

_____

Brambles have overflowed the daffodil fields,
crested the cottage roof.
The paths are lost in mallows, docks and nettles.

Chris Considine, *The Drowning Island*

The young builder who travels down from Bristol with his wife, Amy, a couple of months before we move in, to look at the house and the list of renovation commitments we've made to the Trust, is essentially unsuitable. Bristol is a two-and-a-half-hour drive away, but this is where the couple own a vintage shop and manage a graffiti festival, as well as the building business which has just finished a project in one of the cooler venues of the town. They are younger than us, and much more glamorous. Matt has model good looks and the long legs and confidence of a hound puppy, and it's clear that he's interviewing us, not vice versa. Patrick's father officiated at their wedding, as Amy's family live in the village where he vicars part-time, and got chatting to Matt about eco-builds, and how we are struggling to find a local builder happy to take on a job dependent on tides and weather. Barry, the craftsman of our mainland cottage, comes across to look round, but boggles at the odd hours and the uncertainty of working with the sea.

Matt's eyes, though, start to glint as he looks behind the fireplaces, under the floors, into the broken windows, and Patrick talks him through the plans. We emerge at the far side of the house, on to the lawn where we cut our wedding cake, and gaze expectantly at him.

'Yes,' he decides, slowly, looking up at the house. 'I think I'll take it on.'

My mother, staying with us for a few days in the Looe cottage, comes with us on that island recce with Matt, and for all her affection for the island is aghast at what we've taken on.

'It's far too big a project. It's clearly permanently damp. You'll have to get the water back on – somehow. There are holes in the floor! What about a loo – you can't keep using the one outside. You're both quite mad.'

We have come here too late for my mother. 'It's your fault,' I often remind her. 'You brought us here.' She was 38 when we had our first holiday here, the same age as I am on the day of this visit. Through her forties, she loved the place as fiercely as anyone, but her heart is now in the slopes of Swaledale, though she knows she will soon be leaving them. Climbing on and off the boat is a torture of unbalancing and over-reaching, and even when the house is habitable, the spartan conditions don't meet her modest requirements, in her seventies, for comfort. I hoped that if we were here, if she could spend time here whenever she wanted, it might mitigate the wrench of leaving the Dales. ('It's not just for us,' I tell Patrick, nobly, early on. 'My family . . .') But she looks at the sea, and her mind's eye searches for the patchwork hills.

Timing is tight. Weather dictates that we can't start this project, which depends on transporting people and equipment to and fro across the sea, before March, and we must finish by September. If we are to manage the renovation on the island, to make the house remotely habitable by winter, we conclude that the only option is for us to camp there for those months, bringing our furniture over right at the end for a more comfortable winter. Matt, tickled by the idiosyncrasies of the project, plans to camp too, spending two weeks at a time on the island with his right-hand man, Dave. We are a month ahead of them, starting to strip wallpaper and demolish rotten cupboards in the cold house: we keep a couple of the sisters' armchairs, a couple of their Formica tables, and we have our inflatable bed, our camping stove and the outside loo. We have a wonky light fitting with a bare light bulb which we plug into a long lead running from a single socket in the wiring we're about to strip out. As a very occasional treat we have a few minutes with a fan heater: it would overload the generator, says Patrick, to have it on anything above the lowest setting. Neither our Aga replacement nor the woodburner for the sitting room will arrive until the solar thermal people come to fit our PV solar panels for hot water, and plumb them into a vast copper boiler, and down vast lengths of copper pipes to the back boilers on the two stoves.

We would have loved to keep the old Aga, which pre-dated even the Atkinses' time, temperamental though it was reputed to be. With the wind in the wrong direction, it would not light at all, and, as Gus and Sheila suspected, Babs would then leave the gas poker alight in it to keep it going. At their first Christmas dinner on the island, though, with Babs insisting on cooking, the Aga was filled with festive enthusiasm. While she exchanged Christmas greetings with her guests in the old café room – it was decades by then since any visitor had been in the house – it veered, as it did without warning, from chilly sulks to a scorching blast. As Babs snatched out the carbonised turkey, at least she knew already that Gus and Sheila would laugh until they cried as they excavated for edible scraps, and perhaps next year she would let them cook.

It is almost the first thing we address in the house, given the understanding of the need for heat we gained during our winter trial. It becomes clear very quickly that the Aga cannot be saved; it is rusted beyond repair. Jon tries without success to get it out when he returns from his trip, and when we arrive back on the island in February, Patrick bashes and hacks to shift it from its recess until its internal insulation disintegrates, piling the floor with drifts which overflow the sackfuls we collect. Eventually we bring in a couple of boys from the local builders: they are blasé about the job before they arrive, but are forced in the end to retreat and return with bigger power tools.

We keep warm, then, through that chilly March, by cleaning. In the bathroom, we strip out the mouldy hardboard splashbacks from behind the bath and basin, the decaying boiler cupboard and a lot of flaking paint. We clean out the pantry, or scullery as the sisters knew it, scraping away the paint, scrubbing rust marks from the floor and sweeping and mopping repeatedly: we have visions of slate shelves full of preserves and our own hams hanging from the hooks. We strip the wallpaper from sitting room and kitchen and start to learn about soot, which has coated the fifties pattern of little groups of condiments, so that Patrick has nightmares for the first time in thirty years about the fire which ravaged his prep school and left the classrooms black. The local builders' boys bash out both the old Aga and most of the hideous sitting-room fireplace of purple stone.

Of course this is preparation, clearing, not the persistent, dispiriting battle to keep the house, with its flagstones laid directly on the earth and the outside always trying to come in, in a respectable state. 'Rather squalid,' my mother judges, once the initial work is done and our inconsistent attempts to clean are already failing. Somewhere online, there exists an interview which a helper persuaded Babs to give, sitting at the big oval table in the bay window of what had long ceased to be a café, with Hamilton just out of shot. What, he asked, did she find most difficult about living on the island? What would she pinpoint – the isolation, the physical privations, the fear of incapacitation? 'Housework,' she answered, decisively.

It is bathetic; the least of her worries, one thinks. How could that matter, and why did Babs resist for so long the help which might have made her life easier if only kind friends could have been allowed into the house; surely they would have shrugged at any untidiness? But it only takes a few years for us, two of us in our thirties and forties, to become dismayed by the drifts of dead woodlice in the pantry, the deep dirt camouflaged in the grey flagstones; to be appalled when our friends ask, as they step inside, if they should take their shoes off, and by polite faces as newcomers look about them.

But every time we step out of the house, we can see the sea, and the daily amazements of light and sound and scent. Everything is growing, and the sea is always moving. With the house as cold as the world outside, and far needier, we want to be out as much as we can, and we are both as eager as 17-year-olds with a first car to take out our boat.

For his fortieth birthday, a month after we contacted Callum with our proposal for Island House, Patrick's friends clubbed together to give him an outboard motor: a two-and-a-half horsepower four-stroke Honda. Sailors Graham and Jane gave us the boat, which they no longer used: a little inflatable dinghy, which Graham presented to us in impeccable condition, folded neatly inside its waterproof bag. It was never so neatly stored again.

Earnest, we ask Tony for advice. 'Always stick to the starboard side,' he says, and 'keep well clear of Mid Main. But you'll know,' he adds, with misplaced faith, 'you've been out here often enough.' We drop hints to Ernie to let us steer his boat, but he is far too wise: it takes years for him to trust Patrick enough to allow him to take the tiller, although my four-year-old nephew Gus has it, under benign supervision, the first time he climbs aboard.

The first fine weekend, we manoeuvre our little boat down to the water's edge. It is heavy enough, and awkward to lift, but manageable between the two of us. We have a ship-to-shore radio and paddles, an anchor, a baler and spare fuel. The sun is shining and our spirits are high.

We set off to circumnavigate the island. I leave Patrick to handle the unfamiliar engine and tiller, and perch on top of oars, anchor and pump. It is a thrilling expedition, with the island showing its hidden slopes resplendent with drifts of pink sea thrift, colonies of nesting cormorants, caves and inlets. The boat and engine cope manfully with the sea, which turns out to be rather bigger than we first thought; we realise we have taken on a fair amount of water by the time we are halfway round.

Here, we are out of sight of the land to north-east or west, hidden behind the island, facing nothing but sea. This is what made the island so suitable a stop-off point for smugglers: the Customs men couldn't see them here, and we are also pleased to be out of sight of the telescopes we know are often trained on the island ('I saw you last night,' locals tell us, and we scour our memories for what they might have seen). It's wilder along the south and the west of the island, only the open sea stretching to the end of the world, the shy cormorants and shags nesting on the cliffs, where they expect to be undisturbed.

To the far south-east, beyond Little (or Gull, or Trelawny's) Island, are a group of rocks known as the Ranneys, which we know extend far beyond the visible land. Patrick has steered a good distance out from them before turning back to the west, along the back of the island, and at the furthest point from the rocky shore, the engine dies.

'Let's not panic!' I say, cheerfully. 'This is what the paddles are for!'

'I'm sure it'll come back!' Patrick is equally positive. He tries the engine, a pull-cord, again and again, and it finally sputters back into life.

'Hurrah!' I cheer. 'I'll start baling.'

We have taken on a good deal of water from waves washing over the low sides of the little boat, and the baler and I don't seem to make much impression, but I'm sure it's just a matter of time.

The engine cuts out again after a few yards.

'I'll start rowing,' I decide, but Patrick says, 'Give it a chance, I'm sure we can get it going.'

I lean out of his way as far as possible, to give him space to pull the cord, and try not to overbalance.

'We could call the coastguard?' I suggest.

'I'm sure I can get it started again.'

'I mean, it would be embarrassing, but . . .'

'Better than sinking . . .'

Our teeth are starting to chatter as the engine finally comes back to life. I bale; Patrick coaxes the machinery like a recalcitrant child, given to stopping dead at the end of your arm without warning in the middle of the pavement, and somehow, between us, we will the boat back to the beach.

We are so cold, when we drive up on to the shingle, that not only are feet and limbs struggling, but thought is too. Muttering encouragement to each other, we stagger out, take the boat up the beach and move ourselves slowly up the path towards towels and dry clothes.

There could have been no better introduction to our boating lives, because this teaches us to be conservative. I remember the horror, when I was a child, of a vanished pair of boys from Looe, lost to the sea. Patrick and I have been spoiled by relying on Ernie and the other boatmen, for whom the sea state, the weather, the capabilities of their boats are part of them.

We are not the first island-dwellers to overestimate our seafaring skills. In the early 1880s, a family of three leased the house from the rackety potato merchant Ezra Neale: a married couple and their niece. A reclusive trio, their principal amusement appears to have been porpoise-shooting, which they did from their boat. They drowned near the island in 1883, after a sortie probably not much more ambitious than ours, and no doubt the porpoises laughed. Fifty years or so earlier, young Benjamin Christopher, a better seafarer and engaged in the less contentious process of ferrying lobsters from the island to market, was lost to the sea as well, his body recovered only after his widowed mother took out an advertisement imploring the locals for news.

On an island, water is an Ancient Mariner of a conundrum. Living with the sea, with its dangers and frustrations and wild joy, you are constantly reminded that you are surrounded, lapped by its hugeness and strength. Harnessing the sea on the island's tiny scale is almost impossible, though Patrick dreams of a small desalination plant. The sisters had a temperamental seawater pump which worked at high tide to supply a tank from which we filled buckets to flush the helpers' loo, but by the time Patrick and I arrive, the pipes and equipment are corroded beyond repair.

Conversely, of course, drinking water is always a concern; almost every summer, it is on the point of failing. There is a spring somewhere deep in the rocks, which has been tamed by one of the energetic occupants of the last century and pumped and plumbed into all the buildings. This gives enough water for a population of two, or four, and there is even a bath in Jetty Cottage, but the supply is not sufficient for streams of visitors and helpers. In winter, the sump is overflowing, and pours out of its housing on to the beach, but the water retreats over the summer until the sump is dry, and we're down to our last tank of water . . . We don't realise until we move here that Attie cut off the main water pipe to the house with a hacksaw, in the drought summer of 1976, so that she and Babs, through their seventies and eighties, were as dependent on the single tap in the café, and the helpers' loo, as we were.

For a brief period, mid century, seawater was pumped up and used more extensively, and the occupants of the house and the two cottages would have had the luxury of seawater baths and flushing lavatories. The art-deco bathroom in the house must have been stunning then: it is still lovely, and we restore it with love. The cast-iron bath is re-enamelled, the original taps and shower hose painstakingly renovated; the floor tiled in black and white and the wall behind the bath covered with huge, beautiful glass tiles in pale green with a simple deco design picked out in black. We hope that whoever did put the bathroom in would be pleased. For fifty years or more since they did so, a bath was a distant dream on the island. Jon the warden set up an old cast-iron one on the croquet lawn, with a fire underneath it and willow screens giving a modicum of privacy, but regulating the water temperature proved problematic. Patrick designs a hot-water system for the house which is fed by solar panels and the solid-fuel stoves, connected with yards of copper piping to a huge tank upstairs and radiators around the house. Small electric pumps, powered by the battery bank, deliver rain or spring water to the tank, our thermal store. There is a filtration system for the rainwater to the bathroom, as it's prohibited, we discover, to pipe unfiltered rainwater for washing due to the potential risks, such as legionnaires' disease. A candlelit bath in the art-deco bathroom becomes a preposterous winter luxury.

As children, we spent half our time in the summer sea, and never thought about washing. Later, and visiting in colder weather, there was a laborious process of filling containers from rainwater butts, boiling kettles, and emptying washstands into buckets which then needed manhandling outdoors. Our early weeks living in the house, before the pipework is reconnected, work in the same way: we have a five-litre container of water in the kitchen for drinking and cooking, and use kettles of rainwater from the many water butts for washing and washing up. To preserve water as far as we can, we reuse the contents of our hot-water bottles, pouring them back into the rainwater kettle to re-boil: it is essential to have something to moderate the chill of the bed, but we couldn't contemplate squandering a whole kettleful of fresh rainwater every night.

We have an underpowered camping stove for kettles, but Sheila and Gus bring up a triumphant piece of kit for cooking: a Remoska. It is essentially an inverted electric frying pan, a product of the Cold War communist era with its demand for cheap cooking facilities among the families of Eastern Europe. It developed something of a cult following in the UK, and with Atkinsonian zeal for a gadget, Gus and Sheila snapped one up:

the small size means low power consumption, so, they reasoned, it should be ideal for island use.

Before our cooker arrives, the Remoska is a godsend. It is at its best for poaching and baking; too much moisture, we discover, for a satisfying roast potato. Sheila and Gus gamely join us for meals within days of our arrival in March: the Remoska can't, of course, be used at the same time as the little heater, but switching between them by the light of the electrician's inspection lamp, huddled with Edward and the cats, our social gatherings are cosy islands in the encroaching building site. Our generally traumatised cats are remarkably brave with Edward, the eccentric basset hound: they watch him closely but manage not to run away or even growl.

Exclaiming over a culinary gadget in poor light, accompanied by cats and dogs: those suppers are reminiscent of many parties with Babs and Attie, who adored their fondue set, pancake- and pie-makers.

The dream for both cooking and heating is a range cooker, though, and having failed to rescue the Aga, we order an English-made, purportedly 'greener' version: an Esse. Transport is the great challenge here – getting half a ton of cast iron on the boat and off the boat is not going to be a simple matter of manual lifting. We ask around for a pontoon – there used to be one in the long-vanished boathouse on the island; there used to be one in Looe; didn't someone offer something like that not so long ago – but nothing is available now. We have a protracted dialogue with the local naval base: wouldn't it be a splendid training exercise, we suggest, to drop off the half-ton stove by helicopter? But despite some encouraging noises, this is ultimately decreed to be an exercise of no value.

Eventually, we opt for more old-fashioned methods. We can hire the fish-market crane to deliver the Esse to the *Islander*, the Trust's current boat, with a flap-down front for easy access, and then beach the boat on the island at low tide. With enough manpower, Patrick calculates that it'll then be possible to lever the stove off the boat with lengths of wood, steeply uphill as it won't fit through the *Islander*'s narrow gangway, and on to Jon's tractor. Along with the trio of men overseeing the Esse's installation, we rope in Big Dave, who manages the Trust's farm a few miles away, and Operation Esse commences.

When Patrick and I try to move so much as a heavy shelf together, we are bad-temperedly snapping at each other within minutes, so when Sheila and I go down to the beach to spectate, I am impressed by the scene. While calm men stand around like fielders on a cricket ground, making occasional quiet suggestions, the metal box is poised six feet above ground on a complex system of planks of wood. Gus has been keeping a close eye on the process all morning, and reports that there hasn't been so much as a cross word. The building of the Pyramids suddenly seems comprehensible.

The Esse lands gently, without a scratch, on the flat bed of the big trailer, and Jon's tractor makes nothing of transporting it up the hill to the house. Ingenuity and endurance might have been stretched too far without it, and I rethink my fantasy of replacing the diesel workhorse with Exmoor ponies and a wooden cart.

In situ, the stove looks lovely: a deep royal blue in the alcove neatly tiled by Patrick in the ice-cream, nod-to-the-fifties colours of our kitchen. In use, it is an utter menace, dribbling and then spewing tar and black water from several orifices. We try a number of different chimney cowls, and feed it a number of different types of wood-based fuel, but, like so much island hardware, the cowls simply seize up in the terrific winds and the sea-drenched air. By the time we fix it up with an aerodynamic version with no moving parts, which improves matters for a while, the company who embarked so cheerfully on this, and on the wider solar thermal project to which the Esse contributes to provide heating and hot water, have made far more trips to the island than they were planning and remove us firmly from their Christmas card list.

The range remains, despite the latest cowl, a demanding and whimsical beast. Jon coppices wood from the hundreds of sycamores which have sprung up across the island, chops and splits the logs and delivers them to our garden. We stack the wood laboriously, eventually hitting on the solution of supermarket storage trolleys, six-foot-high cages with metal frames, and fill a dozen of these each year. Every day in winter, we load a couple of wheelbarrows with logs, shaking out the spiders and hundreds of woodlice overwintering in the elegant heap. We cart the logs down to the house, where we feed the voracious range until it consents to heat the thermal store and, from there, radiators around the house. We clean it often, sweeping the chimney with a handsome set of brushes, burning off the tar which collects in the throat of the chimney, scraping and brushing the insides clean. You can spend hours on this at a weekend, and find it choked again by the end of the week.

A few years after the optimistic installation, I spend a couple of days alone on the island. Returning to a cold house, I feed the stove with quantities of wood, and ignore the smoke alarm, even the carbon monoxide alarm which shrieks all morning one day, until at lunchtime I start to throw up and decide that it's more important to be alive than warm. I have a headache which lasts for days, and abandon use of the range until we finally find a visitor – they always come in the end – with the skills, strength and patience to tame the beast, at least for a while.

Electricity is as important as warmth: candles and early nights are all very well – who needs electric light? – but we need to run power tools, and computers. Given the difficulties of finding a general builder, we are relieved that there is already an electrician in Looe who is unfazed by the island: Bob, an ex-trawlerman who was at school with Tim the boatman. He has an uncanny knack of accurate weather-forecasting, and is unconcerned by the vicissitudes of tide and sea swell. He takes on the burden of judging these, of reorganising dates and boats to come over and rewire, to reset the house for a new dawn of power.

We have come here on a 'clean energy' ticket: the possibilities and conundrums of wind and solar speak to the engineer in Patrick, and his passion for new technologies. The Wildlife Trust have rejected the possibility of a wind turbine on the island: offshore and exposed, there would be no shortage of wind to drive it, but they conclude that there's too much risk to bird life from large sails high on the island. Later in our first year, though, Patrick orders a small-scale version, something you might have on a large boat. We fix this ourselves to the back of the house: it looks rather sweet and toy-like there, white wings against a blue sky, but at the first real blow – not really a gale – it becomes enormously overexcited. It strains at its fixings and starts to pull its heavy-duty bolt out of the side of the house; it is just below our bedroom, and Patrick lies awake thinking of it pulling free, breaking through the wall and slicing our heads off in bed.

We take it down, mindful of health and safety, and embark on the bigger project of setting it up independent of the house. It is to be mounted on a metal post, which is on its own very nearly too heavy for the two of us to walk from a horizontal to a vertical position. Coming off the post are four heavy metal cables, each of which is to be fixed into a pit of a cubic metre, filled with home-made concrete – builders' cement and beach sand. With the help of Patrick's father, Vernon, here on a visit, we grimly dig our way through the slatey ground at those four points, with spades and trowels and the heavy, pointed pole Jon uses to put in gateposts. Our spades continually come up against something immoveable – stone, heavy roots – and it is a long time before we can progress to bringing up barrowloads of sand, to mix with cement and rainwater and fill the holes. Vernon is long gone by the time the holes are filled and the metal eyes to receive the cables can be fixed into them, and Gus and Sheila's son and grandson are volunteered for the erection: when the wind turbine is complete, heavy head attached to the vast metal pole, it is literally unmanageable for the two of us. All our strength and hernia-risking effort can't quite get it vertical, going hand over hand, never mind hold it still while the guy ropes are attached to the eyes in the concrete pads, but with the two men to help, we see the turbine raised triumphantly to the sky

'Main-tain-ance!' Ernie warns us, as he follows the saga over its months to completion. 'It's all about the main-tain-ance!'

It lasts for three days before the converter breaks. Patrick concludes that the turbine head isn't big enough for the amount of wind and we can't afford a new one; but for those three days, whizzing like a Catherine wheel, it looks superb.

The system Patrick has planned is to store all the electricity we generate – by wind, by solar, or by generator top-ups – in vast batteries, which will allow us to access electricity 24 hours a day. Living here with Patrick and his technical solutions is very different from staying in the various huts when the sisters were in the house, when we washed with kettles of rainwater, ate only food which could survive unchilled, could use electricity only for a few hours in the evening, and, of course, in those pre-internet, pre-mobile days, had no means of communicating with the outside world. As the electrical and plumbing systems are refined, the only reminder that these are not mains services is the tendency for problems: the rainwater dries up, the spring-water tank rusts through and empties; the batteries fail.

The first batteries, to be fair to them, are not really designed to last: though they seem huge and vastly heavy (I can only just lift one), they are apparently small and puny, experimental batteries to deal with the initial electrical ambition for night-time lighting. They are succeeded by second-hand batteries from forklift trucks, which are impressively vast, around three feet high and solid, before we finally invest in some 'redheads', which are a more modest size and jauntily capped in scarlet. Patrick cherishes these immensely, feeding them distilled water and dashing around to seek the culprit when his monitor tells him that an unwise electrical load is troubling them. Ernie's cries of 'Main-tain-ance!' have finally impressed themselves on him, and the redheads remain dependable. 'We now have,' he boasts, '345 AH of storage . . . Since installation, we have generated 21 kW of solar power, and consumed 6 kW of generator power – so almost 80 per cent of our electricity demands have been met by solar to date.' Few things please him more than shaking his head in horror when someone on the mainland tells him what their electricity consumption is, and he is able to boast of ours.

Babs and Attie would have been astonished. In their time, a succession of more or less moody Lister generators provided the power for the island buildings: the house, the cottages, the helpers' huts, the generator and tractor sheds, Attie's pottery and studio. For years, the sisters would walk the hundred yards along the path four times a day, often in the dark, to the shed beyond Smugglers Cottage, where they could switch the generator on or off with the turn of a key. Someone's bright idea (perhaps their predecessors, the Whitehouses, who led quiet, orderly lives here except for the horror of the monkeys) was to fix the generator to start if any light was turned on anywhere on the island. For the Atkinses, with hundreds of helpers and holidaymakers over the summer, this was a maddening problem as sleepy individuals pressed switches without thinking in the middle of the night. The helpers' loo had long since had its light switch decommissioned, and there were fierce warnings, when I was a helper, to remember to turn off the master switch at the back of Jetty Cottage, where Jon now keeps his firewood, by half past ten at night to disable all lights in the cottage, the Chalet and the huts.

Later, a magisterial metal box was installed in the house, from where a suitably heavyweight switch could be thrown without recourse to the generator shed. This is still *in situ* when we arrive, rusty but impressive, but neither it nor the rest of the house's wiring is really usable or safe.

Bob and his mate stay for a few nights when they start work, housed by Jon and Claire in Jetty Cottage – they gracefully decline our offer of Remoska cooking, and sleeping bags in the dust and darkness. They are cheerful through the days reliant on our feeble camping-gas kettle and the insalubrious outside bucket-flush loo, and we're all relieved that when darkness falls, they can enjoy the luxuries of Jetty Cottage: warmth, light, and football on television.

At the end of the week – the old wiring stripped out, Patrick's new design in and connected via armoured cable to the generator – we prepare for a grand switch-on, and realise it has not occurred to us to buy light bulbs.

Chapter 8

Logistics

Faith is setting off in an open boat
into emptiness (the boatman
promising nothing).

Chris Considine, *Setting Out*

Before the builders start in March that first year, we have a long session with Tim, the official island boatman, who brings day visitors in the summer, bird-ringers from the Trust, and the local group who come monthly to watch for seals. With any build or renovation, there is a complex dance to co-ordinate, of labour and trades and equipment, and this one must be set to the music of tides and weather forecasts, and interspersed with the steady footfall of those regular visitors. We produce a long and detailed document covering the first few weeks, starting the next day with a huge delivery of building supplies, timber, the composting loo, which will all come straight to the quay to unload on to the boat. This is *Islander*, the Trust's boat, bought for passenger accessibility and to make loading and unloading easy, with its hydraulic ramp allowing you to carry heavy, bulky objects on and off without heaving and stretching from one person to another over the side. Excited in the early-morning drizzle, we meet Matt and Dave on the quay and watch for the lorry. We watch for three hours, taking it in turns to dash towards the bridge when we see a large vehicle coming – 'I think that's him!' – or to phone the suppliers: 'He's on his way.'

We wait a further hour with the driver, a twinkling pirate with a grey ponytail who stands by the lorry talking about ley lines, for Tim, who will oversee loading of the boat.

'Bit of a problem,' Tim greets us. 'A stone in the steering rod. She'll have to go up to Rock to fix.'

We have a hard deadline of September to finish the build, before winter seas render travel plans impossible, and Matt and Dave have only cleared their diaries for a fortnight, but the boat will be out of action for several weeks.

We unload the lorry on to the landlocked boat, because there is nowhere else to put the stuff, and then we go and look for Ernie.

Ernie, agreeing to step into the breach, saves us. He evidently relishes the challenge: he is a man of solutions. While transporting the larger and heavier items we need will be more of a struggle, handing them over the sides of his boat, *Pania*, rather than walking straight up *Islander*'s ramp, the gain of his positivity and expertise far outweighs that loss. In fact the delay of waiting for *Islander* would have made the necessary works to the house simply impossible: we would have had to walk away. In springs to come, crossing to the island in good or bad weather, Ernie reminisces with a quiet pride: 'We were lucky that March, though . . . some stuff we brought over.' He is well into his seventies, but fitter than any of us and expert with the boat in rough seas, treacherous landing conditions, out in all weathers in his oilskins, shaking his head and grinning. He'll go out when the big boats stay in the harbour, when the sea is 'like a washing machine', when you seem to be surfing halfway across, when you're soaked by spray before you get out over the harbour bar. 'I don't know,' he'll say, approaching the island in rough seas, and we say, 'Don't risk it, Ernie, if you don't like the look of it we'll just go back,' but he keeps going, shaking his head and repeating, 'I don't know,' until he's alongside the jetty or holding just off the beach and we've leaped ashore with our bags and are waving him off into the dusk and the storm in his yellow bib and braces.

Within a day or two, we are reloading the timber and other hardware on to *Pania*, along with Mick the gas man and a modest cooker. I am left behind to guard all that wouldn't fit on the first trip, and I wait for a long half-hour on the quay, wistfully watching them head out beyond the harbour mouth, river traffic moving on the calm water in front of me while *Pania* faces a frisky March sea. When Matt and Dave return, they report the first landing 'not as bad as we expected', the second 'a bit wetter': they are soaked to their waists. I finally join the others to unload the last boatful on to the beach; the water is higher, and rougher, and Jon and Claire join the four of us in the breaking waves with the boat swinging about. Mick, having fitted the cooker as best he could in half the time he needed, tears back down the path, in the vanishing window for him to escape to the mainland, as we shout at each other:

'Stop! Let him sort the boat out!'

'Just get it off! Keep going!'

Once we notice Mick, he becomes the focus of the yelling – 'Hurry up! Run! We can't hold the boat straight!' – and he has to dive barefoot into the boat from a riot of seaweed and waves.

Early visitors arrive. My childhood friend Katie is the first, rightly, bringing a bottle of gin, a cream tea, and a leather-bound visitors' book, an echo of a long series of books the sisters insisted everyone must sign. We are both married, now, meeting at this place out of time where we lived out our adolescence with cider and silliness and early boyfriends – Simon, and his heroic swim; Jim, who my mother caught me in bed with one night when she came round with a torch, paranoid about teenage pregnancy in an irony which strikes us both, later.

More unexpectedly, we see Jack Proffitt-White, the handsome teenager with whom I first went to the sisters' cottage at Bassett Court to collect their tins of winter pet food, with whom I stood on the quay in the perfect morning light, waiting for the boat. There were four of the Proffs on the island that summer, plus Jack's girlfriend, blonde and smiling and sweet. I was in love with the whole family, as was my brother John, who met them first on an early solo trip. 'Wreaking havoc with raspberry canes,' he wrote in his ebullient letter home that year, 'the Proffitt-White family are pains!' How else could an Englishman sum up his love for a family which seemed so different from ours: boisterous, practical, cohesive, with an open invitation to us for games of cards, cups of tea, beer while it lasts? They were the stuff of legend to me from John's *Swallows and Amazons* tales of family larks, and I was ecstatic to be here among them: the year before, John had watched me, at 12, crying in the boat after our island stint, and made the stupendous offer that I could come with him the next summer, for an extra week on top of the family holiday. So, 'STREWTH!' as my brother Paul exclaimed in the Atkinses' visitors' book during his first stay, 'I am staying and it is just heaven!'

At 13, I crushed into the Chalet with John and the Profs in the evenings: Ro, who mothered and teased us; her irascible husband Dave, with his violent limp from a motorcycle crash and his persuasive way with the island's rusty machinery; Robin, almost my own age, and therefore almost beneath notice – Ro christened us Pip and Estella when I became too haughty; and Jack, a safe dream, with his happy girlfriend. Dave dried my hair, soft from rainwater, with incongruous tenderness; the boys took John to throw him off the jetty to wash his.

At the end of that holiday, Babs and Attie had a rare night ashore at a book signing, and the Proffs had the honour to be trusted to manage the island for 24 hours. It was a glorious day, and we counted over a hundred visitors, Ro charming them with Babs's stories and Attie's scones. The afternoon high tide brought us one of the great set pieces of island life: a delivery of diesel oil, pushed off the boat in rusty barrels by Tony, guided to the shore and then rolled by all of us up the beach and a stretch of shingle path to the generator shed. The energy of the day fizzed into traditional end-of-stay festivities: a treasure hunt, composed by my brother and skipping us around the island; and fish and chips, picked up on the last trip from Looe and preposterously exotic after a week of John's catering from tins. John himself was delighted to see more tins, because a week of rationing had left both him and Jack longing for beer: the treasure hunt, starting at the jetty, ran on a theme:

My first begins two thirsty men
My second ends 'Ale' – same subject again . . .

Only Lucky, Babs and Attie's courteous brown-and-white dog, took no part in our celebrations, the immense satisfaction of the successful understudies. He sat above the jetty, looking out to sea for their return, until darkness hid the water from him and we could persuade him indoors.

I think it might have been the happiest day of my life, and I was overwhelmed by a shock of grief the next day when everyone else departed and I stayed on for a planned, brave few days alone.

The island was safe enough for my parents to entrust me to it at 13, and Babs looked after me in the best possible way, lending me Tilly, the sociable striped cat, so that I could cry into her fur in the empty hut.

Dave still phones us at Christmas, and asks after the oaks he once planted here. For them all, it is an extraordinary, preposterous thought, as it is for everyone for whom the island still means the sisters, that we are going to live in their house.

Jack remembers, most of all, the shooting stars. Shoring up steep mud paths in the woods with timber-edged steps; laughing through the evenings in the crowded Chalet, while his family were still a unit; pushing my brother off the jetty – 25 years on, he remembers these too, but the marvellous shooting stars stripe through his pictures of the island. His father is alone now in their family home; his mother, remarried in New Zealand; Robin, living in Australia with two children. When we last met, Jack was not long into the army, now he is almost out of it. It seems a lifetime since the shooting stars, and the Chalet is a ruin crammed with junk; the house we are in now still has a frisson of the forbidden.

We have plenty of visitors in the first year, fewer in the second and, as the romance of the island shifts to the reality of inaccessibility and discomfort, the numbers dwindle. We try not to press-gang every visitor into helping with the renovation of the house and the land, but it is more difficult than we expect, and almost everyone who comes makes foolish, generous offers which we always fail to resist.

Our friends Bridget and Keith negotiate a week's absence for their daughter Grace, a strong-willed and beguiling five-year-old whose teachers perhaps don't understand her, and her brother, who is eight and more ready to please. Bridget is wondering whether, perhaps, she might home-school Grace, and brings a wealth of educational material for their stay. The children learn about butterflies and sea creatures, our water systems and the movements of the sea, and Bridget has an insight into the world of teaching.

She and Keith have offered to involve themselves in a Big Project, and we embark with them on the construction of the Great Shed. We have ruined the sheds this replaces, stacking logs against the walls, which bend and belly and become permanently wet; the plan is to take them down, carefully construct a flat floor and rebuild them as one big structure. Between us, we haul every piece of timber for the floor and new frame, every new roof and floor panel, up from the jetty. Although we have just taken delivery of a smart electric barrow, the path to the jetty is narrow and the barrow overbalances on every journey, so we carry each piece of wood up by hand. We spend days and days trying to create a flat base, and talking politely in the gusty air about the challenges of tech start-ups, and the next year they choose another holiday, and Grace stays at school.

Patrick's brother William jokes at a family party about the 'labour camp' of the island, and it is painfully accurate. The island is endlessly thirsty for energy, for action, and we sacrifice our friends and family to its open throat. We make efforts to find mechanical assistance for serious deliveries like the timber, attempting not to take advantage of Jon and his tractor, but these are largely unsuccessful. The front tyre of the smart electric barrow punctures, we discover, every time you look at it in a way it doesn't like, and it spends more time waiting to be fixed than it does in use. The power barrow Patrick builds, using electric wheelchair parts from eBay for the 'power' and a long wooden pallet for the bed, ends up so heavy that when the electrical controller fails (after a couple of rather wild trips: the steering needs some work), the barrow is completely unusable, and joins the queue waiting to be fixed. We manhandle over a mini tractor of our own, which rusts and dies under a metal pig ark, and even when a mechanically minded friend bodily takes the engine away and oversees the apprentice at work fixing it up, the winter kills it again. The sisters had shedfuls of decayed machinery, rusted and ruined by the salt and the damp, and now we understand why. It takes concentration and endless maintenance to keep anything metal here, and we are slapdash; we abuse human assistance instead.

For the initial, serious work on the house, we have budgeted for paid labour, and Matt and Dave come at its demands with determination. They have decided, optimistically, to camp for their first fortnight here. They proudly erect their 'mess tent' halfway up the hill, with a lovely view, but by the time they return to it in the evening to forage for food, they find it's blown away. We are relieved to persuade them, in blustery March, to abandon camp and sleep among the seed potatoes sprouting in the main bedroom of the house. Attie too made the chitting of potatoes a priority, when the sisters and their ally Ruth moved to the island early in 1965, and I am pleased by the continuity, though the potatoes do take up much of the boys' living space.

It's just as well that Patrick's business is still at the 'development' stage and he is not a slave to his desk for a solid eight hours a day. He and Justin are encouraged by their first clients, and still buoyed enough by house sales and buyouts, and exhausted enough by what preceded them, not to panic about increasing revenue: working days can be flexible. Patrick goes virtuously to his desk for 9 a.m., but is usually out within the hour to involve himself with the building project of the day. He has a finger in every pie.

In several trips over the summer, Matt and Dave build ceilings and patch the rat-holes in floorboards; they insulate and plaster and render. Early on, they fit the compost loo, with the 'compost' chamber in the old boiler room, below the bathroom, where Babs made her dainty sandwiches for trippers; the wall which carved out a space for the helpers' loo is demolished. They extract a fifties Italian sink from the boiler room, and plumb this into the kitchen; they fit a shower above the bath upstairs, and plumb in the reclaimed basin. We reconnect the water, and rejoice. They dig in a system of pipes for our grey water; they finish stripping back the purple beach stones of the sitting-room fireplace, and the green Edwardian hearth tiles beneath, to find a quiet granite fireplace, which they shore up with a new lintel, a lovely piece of sweet chestnut from Jon. They battle with solar panels in high winds, and fail to catch anything in their many, always optimistic, fishing trips in our little inflatable boat.

The solar panels are particularly dear to Patrick's heart. The Trust have already put in place solar thermal panels for water heating, on the roofs of both Jetty and Smugglers Cottage. We position ours on the flat roof above the bathroom; this part of the house is such an ugly, brutal, square extension, next to the angular interest of the rest of it, that we think the slope of the panels rather enhances the architecture. By happy coincidence, it is also the south-west corner of the house, where they will absorb the maximum amount of sun.

Patrick spends uncharacteristically patient hours coaxing power cables under the stairs, across the hall ceiling, through the bedroom floor, down into the corner of the sitting room. Despite the inefficiency of this long and winding cable, he has opted to house the monstrous batteries and most of the control gear in the old boiler room, his new office: they need good ventilation, and the boiler room is almost an outhouse, with its thin, post-war walls, so the ventilation is really draught.

The PV – electricity-generating – panels are installed by Matt and Dave, grim in a rainstorm, on the roof of one of the house's odder extensions: a bay window at the back, facing away from the sea and into the rise of the hill behind it, which adds perhaps four feet to half of the sitting room and houses the 'secret room' above. We've always been intrigued by the mysterious secret room, with its little windows at either end but no access, and are disappointed when we finally get a ladder and peer in from the outside to find nothing in there but a dead pigeon. We knew the old stories that it was used to signal to ships: if a lamp was lit in the secret room, then the coast was clear for the smugglers. It seems a delightful mystery, until one starts to rationalise (how would you get a light in there, with the windows fixed and no other access, though of course it's not clear how the pigeon got in either). We learn to leave mysteries alone, despite the intriguingly hollow-sounding flagstone in the kitchen floor, and to embrace Attie's philosophy that it is more diverting not to pin down all puzzles to the often prosaic truth.

One of the secret room's secrets is whether or not it houses bats. The Trust insist that a bat expert comes to survey it; this can't happen until the bats are active enough, in May, so until then we can't disturb the slates or the fascia boards or stray into the roof void. Drilling through the slates is allowed, apparently, so during the builders' first trip, the rails to hold the panels are fixed on with foot-long bolts, and despite the ladders being repeatedly blown off the roof, the PV solar panels are finally attached. That night, for the first time, we keep the lights on after 10 p.m.

Triumph, however, is toppled by toast. We are excited about running an electric toaster again: we have been using a gas-ring version, on which you perch slices of bread like a house of cards, but we find that the toast simply refuses to brown. Dave is prepared to eat it, and it is warm and vaguely crisp, but it doesn't have the colour, the robustness, the crunch of proper toast. Smug in the luxury of PV, we press the slider on the electric toaster down for the first time and watch the elements against the bread light up, only to go immediately dark again. The toaster has tripped the inverter, the middleman between batteries and power source, and our elegant electrical system fails.

Patrick manages to negotiate replacement of the faulty component without losing his temper with the manufacturer's technical support ('Have you tried turning it off and turning it on again?'), and it negotiates the volcanic ash storm between it and us to bring us renewed power on demand, to run the many small power tools – sanders, drills – which sound around the house daily. We are able to run a fridge (in itself, an improbable luxury here) all day, rather than in line with the generator; someone leaves a light on all night, and the new system survives. In the spring sunshine, we find ourselves independent of the generator altogether and feel the first, smug glow of self-sufficiency.

Solar power is a luxury for us, given that the generator exists, rather than the transformational source of energy that allows rural parts of developing countries to cast aside their kerosene lamps and embrace the revolution of constant light and power. It is an obvious next step, though, for the island: to escape the reliance on the diesel oil the generator needs – the expense, the strain of delivery, the environmental contraindications – and run instead on sunshine. Patrick is full of enthusiasm for the lateral thinking which off-grid living requires, and full of relish for this new technology. Personally, I am delighted to be able to put a light on at night.

As the church bells are ringing on Easter Sunday, Patrick and I pause our scraping and sanding, tiling and painting, and put down the Nitromors, sugar soap and steel wool. The boys and long-suffering Ernie fetch over a boatload of plasterboard and insulation, and we sit then in the afternoon sun in the airing Atkins armchairs and read the *Observer* in the luxury of the calm after the storm, the four of us congratulating ourselves on a job well begun. That Easter sees our first party in the house, on makeshift furniture, with Matt and Dave, Gus and Sheila, an ambitious goose.

On their last night, we are overtaken by the dark as the generator goes to bed before us, but the boys stay up with head torches to finish shingling in between the slates on the hearth, and Ant the cat stays with them for moral support. She has developed a passion for Dave: she is always the sociable cat, an expressive paw pushing attention-grabbing laptops away, stroking a face or casually stealing food from a plate, and she snuggles on to his lap now whenever he sits down. We miss the boys' energy when they go, as well as the sense of irresistible progress, but Ant misses the moments of stillness.

Ant's love for Dave does not ameliorate the cats' sense of deep disturbance as the days and weeks of building work progress, and they form an alliance they haven't had since kittenhood, when eight tiny paws tickled their way around my house: the solace of the single girl. I find them now in different cupboards around the house, one on the upper shelf, one on the lower, keeping very still and quiet so the monsters won't notice them. Patrick grumbles when they burrow into the centre of the bed, and complains about the smell.

'They don't smell!' I insist. 'What do they smell of?'

'Animal,' he replies, irrefutably, but he understands that they are family, and the only time I ever hear him unselfconsciously use a term of endearment is with Bee.

'What's the matter, dear?' he asks her, when she's sadder than usual, and in the early months she is often sad. The house is a horror of drilling and upheaval, and the wideness of outdoors, grass beaten by the sea-winds, stumps them both after their tame London garden. When we first let them out, they sit on the doorstep and stare at the cold expanse of scrub and rock and sea, and dare no further. Gradually, after many nights of coaxing them from under bushes where only Patrick's collar-fixing gadget (the Loc8tor: 'pinpoint directional technology!') can find them, they come to terms with this new world, but they are careful not to stray dangerously far from home. Bee finds a new tormentor in the shape of a blackbird, who has no doubt that the territory is his and chases her indoors with musical shouts and curses.

This is embarrassing for her, but nothing to the urban brutality of Pussolini, the black cat owned by the Italian next door to us in London. After he broke in through even our security cat flap, Bee left home and was only found after a fortnight and a leafleting campaign, hiding out two streets away. He had evidently bitten her as she fled, and infection had got into an ignominious but nearly fatal wound on her flank. Emergency Sunday surgery saved her, but when we let her out after several weeks indoors, she vanished within days, back to the neighbour's garden and its little cave under a shed: at least we knew where to find her. She wasn't cut out for the turf wars of city life.

Now, she has only Ant to bully her. Although William, Gus and Sheila's ratting cat, follows his owners on walks around the island until just before his death, enormous to the end in his cloud of striped fur, he leaves our immediate territory to our cats. They seem impervious to the ghosts of previous island cats: Tilly, my childhood companion, and her sister Samantha, the Atkinses' 'talking cat', shy in her tortoiseshell fluff. In the late evening, you might catch her conversing with Babs in the cooling gardens, or see a glimpse of short-haired, silver Sue moving between the stone monkeys along the battlemented wall. Before them were the three kittens the Atkinses named after island smugglers, Hamram, Joan and Bessie; and earlier still, Cleo, the Whitehouses' cat, spent six months here alone once her owners left, a sentry in the rafters of the tractor shed.

But the island is no longer privately owned, and on an official nature reserve, cats excite comment; more so when the rats they helped to control have all gone in the Trust's concerted cull. Jon the warden has been clear about his concerns from our first meeting about the house – but for us the cats are non-negotiable; 'a deal breaker', Patrick explained. The Big Cheese at the Trust seemed relaxed about them, but Jon was the one trying to manage the island and he remained seriously unconvinced. 'The last thing we would want to do', we emailed him after the meeting, 'is undermine your good work. We are absolutely open to any compromise suggestions you might have, but ultimately if we can't find a workable solution, it may be the best thing for the island for us to bow out.'

We are ready to. From the beginning we have been waiting for the decisive blow to our improbable plans: for the Trust to say no in our first phone call; for Jon to say no in our second; for the lawyers to come up with something insurmountable; for our spartan winter test run to be unmanageable. But as the building work progresses, there is still no decisive negative, so we offer compromises for the cats: collar bells, a curfew, a variety of patent deterrents for Claire's more prized flower beds. Then a local wildlife group start a flurry of emails; they are 'shocked & angry at the presence of new cats on Looe Island which is a nature reserve & bird sanctuary. This situation is intolerable,' they protest.

Naively, it hadn't occurred to us that there would be opposition to us living quiet lives on the island; we'd thought that if we could agree plans with the Trust then the difficulties would be within us, with isolation, a precarious new business, dwindling funds. We are distressed by the response of this group, with whom we thought we were on good terms, and by some other antagonism we encounter in our first months. But the island brings out an extraordinary sense of ownership in people: it is special, remarkable, a private delight to so many that the most casual day visitor talks wistfully of their nightly dreams of the place, and whole books have been written about a single stay. The local people are less sentimental and do not comment; they have seen island-settlers come and go, and they know that we will go too in due course.

It is an odd relationship, the island with the mainland. We find it almost impossible to create a social life, or join a group, in Looe or Liskeard, with tide and weather so unpredictable. We slowly develop friendly acquaintances, and feel a deep satisfaction from the casual chats and greetings which start to be a feature of time spent in Looe. We long, after city anonymity, for a sense of community, but are inevitably isolated by the half-mile of sea.

At the same time, we are more dependent than most on local people and institutions: the patient staff of the harbour commissioners, who put up with absurd deliveries (a shed, a tractor) to the harbour office, and often have them in the way for far too long before we collect them. The lifeboat crew might quite possibly one day save our lives: taken ill on the island, capsized at sea.

And Ernie, who is essential not only to the success of the renovation, but to our lives on the island: he'll come out if he possibly can, in almost any weather; he'll collect prescriptions from Boots, bring us emergency gin, pull our car out of stone gutters I've wedged it into. Margaret, his wife, waits in for our deliveries, helps out at no notice with our first attempt at plucking poultry, and brings us chocolate eggs one Easter when Patrick is ill ashore. Together, they drive for three hours in a storm to safely relocate a crateful of ducks when I'm stuck in the cottage too sick to get out of bed, and then arrive at the door the next day to nurse me. 'Any time of the day or night,' he tells us, 'I'll be there.'

Chapter 9

Progress

Children have grown here, shed their childhoods, gone.
Love has been found; bathed in like phosphorescence
in midnight water; lost. And all the past is a blur
of superimposed transparencies.

Chris Considine, *Endings*

I didn't go into the woods on the island much as a child, only really if a brother took me. I wanted the brightness of beaches, the openness of windswept grassland. We came at the wrong time of year, then, to see the woodland paths glitter suddenly with primroses and violets, then shine with swathes of wild garlic and bluebells. In summer, the dark sycamore canopy unnerved me, and there were strange, oversized relics: a collapsed hammock, like a giant's string vest; the huge, ivy-covered bomb crater where the wartime parachute mine was dropped, shattering greenhouse windows along the seafront at Looe; and the sad remains of henhouses.

What happened to those hens, why Babs and Attie abandoned their pursuit of fresh eggs, I never heard, but they didn't respond well to helpful suggestions from visitors that chickens were just what they needed. For us, producing eggs, like vegetables, is an achievable step towards the kind of self-sufficiency that the Atkinses wanted, and in our first spring on the island, all three households turn their minds to the procurement of egg-laying birds.

Claire chooses chickens, but I'm not keen on their scratchy feet and pecky beaks, and we decide to go in with Gus and Sheila on some ducks. Claire loves her hens, and she and Gus both hold conversations with them – white Wilma; Big Bad Bertha, a bullish speckled grey; and mild-mannered brown Betty – in a combination of words and squawks. Over the years, looking after successive chickens when Jon and Claire are away, I gradually warm to them, to their inquisitiveness and small crooning noises, but I always prefer the ducks, who run out to meet us when we've been away, who stay up late on the lawn long after the chickens have gone to bed, who meet a rainstorm with open wings instead of running for shelter and grumbling, and who lay bigger, richer eggs.

My brother Paul, visiting from Australia in our first summer as island residents, builds 'Duckingham Palace' with his wife, Jay, from the muddle of doors and windows discarded from the house. Gus, the expert in woodworking, advises them, and they produce a long, narrow house with a pitched roof, complete with skylight. Poring over the 1940s handbook, *Keeping Poultry and Rabbits on Scraps*, we have concluded that Khaki Campbells will be the best layers, although we add Indian Runners for Gus – 'They look so funny when they run' – the following year.

Happily, it is also Paul who drives to the farm a few miles away on the mainland to collect the three Khaki Campbells we find: looking at the map, I recognise the nearest village as the one I walked to to find help, or a phone signal, after I'd followed the satnav, coming home from a shopping trip with Sheila, into a deeply rutted farm track, which eventually stuck on the car's undercarriage and halted progress completely. Sheila spent an hour in the stationary car, whose windows I'd left open, working out how to keep herself warm overnight if I never returned from phoning the AA. 'I've got an elderly passenger!' I told them, but I knew this was absurd: Sheila would survive the apocalypse long after I would.

Sheila and Gus, dogged in their devotion to the island, provide a gentle stability in its transition from the character it has with Babs and Attie there – a place of remarkable women; a story of luck and dreams and bravery – to its new, more impersonal life as a wildlife reserve. This makes all the difference to us, and our ability to continue our relationship with the place, but is also gold to the TV researchers who come to recce the island for a segment of the BBC's *Coast* and are wowed by the white-haired couple in the chocolate-box cottage. Sheila leans over the gate to chat to them, invites them into the garden; they can't stop listening to her uncontrived confidences, marvelling at her matter-of-fact acceptance of the demands and privations of island living. They look around at the island cast, talk briefly to Jon and Claire about wildlife, the Trust, but can't resist Sheila, her warm voice with its island stories, the cottage's sunny garden. She is unfazed by the cameras, and they spend longer than they'd intended here, soothed by the idyll as they film.

When we watch the episode, it is a completely satisfying few minutes of television. Gus has a supporting role with some runner beans, and the dogs nudge and dash their way into shots, but it is Sheila who communicates the place.

Attie, Babs and Sheila were unexpected exponents of island life: 'the most unlikely would-be islanders', as Attie described herself and Babs. All three of them, though, were natural raconteurs, fascinating lenses through which to examine the question which seems to go so sharply to the heart of most visitors: what's it like to live on an island? People are polarised by the remoteness, either 'I can't think of anything worse' or 'I can't think of anything better.' It is self-contained and tiny in an increasingly huge world. Globalisation makes us, and Jon and Claire, more connected with the rest of the world; the four of us leave the island far more than previous occupants, and Gus and Sheila's ability to survive without doing so (or wanting to) is part of what appeals to the makers of *Coast*.

*

The three ducks which Paul brings back from South Muchlarnick are plump and brownish: Patrick names Bill, deaf to complaints that this is no name for a girl; Sheila, the Harry Potter aficionado, names Hermione; and Gus is happy for me to name the third duck Penguin. They are delighted by their house, but, like Legolas, Hermione is undone by the proximity to the sea. After a couple of weeks in the garden of Smugglers Cottage, the great water calls to her, and she leaves her sisters and Duckingham Palace. We soon locate her, a particularly noisy quack on Jetty Beach, and see her too, swimming with the wild mallards. She has no interest in the food with which we try to tempt her, and lives the rest of her life on the beach and in the water, surfing the wash in and out, between the rocks. Penguin dies quietly, without warning – in the manner of fowl – after a year, but Bill is the matriarch for many years, living to a grand old age among her changing family.

Both my brothers visit this first summer here: Paul, the builder of Duckingham Palace, from Australia with his Australian wife and sons, and John from Canada with his Canadian family: both of my brothers were Thursday's children. We were last together two years ago, while our father was dying, and it is a relief to slide into this place of holidays, with its creative preoccupations of food and renovation.

Paul's family are squashed together on motley mattresses in the spare bedroom, while John's are housed in the Trust's new tipi, magnificent halfway up the hill. Although, some months in,

I still feel a twinge of guilt every time I walk into the house, and particularly up the stairs into territory which has always been so completely forbidden, for Paul the sense of trespass may be less. He is one of the very few people from the time of our relationship with the Atkins sisters to have come right inside the house, as far as the sitting room, for the sisters found themselves on television during that long and lonely holiday when Paul was 16, and invited him in. Attie's second book must recently have been published, and both newspaper articles and TV appearances were relatively frequent, but novel enough to celebrate and share.

Paul was overwhelmed, he remembers, by the sheer quantity of belongings and projects crammed in here: dozens of demijohns of home-made wine, piles and piles of books, dogs and cats, papers and pottery, blankets and shells and boots: rooms so crammed with stuff that it was difficult to negotiate a path through it. Kath, an Atkins favourite – indefatigable in the gardens, stalwart in spring-cleaning, wise enough not to advance opinions – describes the same abundance: a sense of the people and the house bubbling to overflowing like a demijohn bursting its bung; strange, restless movement even under the blanket on Attie's lap, bulges which appeared and then vanished, until two cats emerged and the exuberance of the blanket subsided.

Kath comes back to visit decades later, still tireless among the vegetables, pointing out the dolphins in the bay. She and

John's wife Sylvia are both blessed, on their different visits, by the magic of watching the silver leap and curve and dive, and they both deserve it.

For my nephews, it is their first visit, and it is the first meeting of the cousins. Finbarr is three and a half now, and his brother Aengus only fifteen months, constantly thwarted this summer from exploring cliffs and sea, flagstones and builders' rubble, by a sturdy travel cot. Nicholas is a precocious ten-year-old, bitterly disappointed when Uncle Paul is the only one on their fishing trip to catch, at Ernie's direction, the glorious silver bass. He reminds me of Paul at the same age, avid with a shrimping net at the turn of the tide, determined to return with enough of a catch to eat.

Patrick and I have so far failed to catch a single fish on the island, although Patrick's brother Willy catches a wrasse from Landing Beach. These are the other end of the scale from delicious bass, which go for £25 and more at the fish shop; wrasse are greenish and bony and never seen in fishmongers. Willy is determined to prepare and cook his, and we eat it in a small, surprisingly edible fish pie, impressed by his achievement.

I used to catch reasonable quantities of prawns when I was a child, but they don't seem plentiful now. Babs would occasionally lead us to the beach with shrimping nets at the turn of the tide, and make us prawn cocktails with the catch in the evening. Paul catches enough for a sandwich on one trip, but he is as unsuccessful as we are in catching crabs in the lobster pots which we try in various places; the boys who come in our first spring to replace the rotten windows are the only people who see anything in their optimistic pots. We send various parties fishing with Ernie, and they are always successful: Paul's sea bass takes the prize for quality, and Patrick's young godson Tom wins on quantity, with a terrific haul of pollack, mackerel and whiting, which he and his friend are disturbingly eager to bash on the head, and just about prepared to eat.

Those two boys are the naughtiest visitors we have, although a nephew and his friends, a few years later, provoke a call to the Trust from an unnamed complainant to say that they have been tipping seagulls out of their nests. There is a photograph in one of Attie's books of a helper mending the seawater pump, willy-nilly on the cliffs where the herring gulls nest, holding a metal dustbin over his head for protection as the adult birds attack. We give the gulls a very wide berth when they have eggs or young; they dive-bomb viciously if you come within yards of them, and on reflection we agree with the nephew that approaching their nests deliberately might be quite a self-limiting sport: 'We're not that stupid!' he convinces us.

When Tom visits, we give the boys a small video camera of Patrick's and tell them to make a film, in the hope of keeping them out of trouble, but they come back with only a few images of themselves, poised terrifyingly on cliffs. The main rule we've given them is not to kill themselves, and they do, just, stick to that, but anything else is fair game. 'Anyone who comes here and doesn't go coasteering', writes Tom's friend in our visitors' book, 'is MENTAL!' They have clambered their way up and down and around the cliffs of the island's west side, around the caves of High Cove, in and out of the sea. This is forbidden territory now, with more formal wildlife protection in place, and we scold them roundly; but we see the attraction too.

To reach, from the land, the caves of High Cove, which are on the wild side of the island to the south-west, where the cormorants and shags nest and dry their wings, there are two possible routes: a vertical climb down the cliffs which form the eastern side of the caves, or a longer clamber over the rocks from Dunker Point to the north-west. There are rumours that there is a labyrinth, not so far under the island's surface, of elaborate caverns of prehistoric design and brick construction, but I only ever find sea-scored rock hollows under the cliff, housing bats and darkness.

The only person I know who really understands those descents is my brother John, who consented, one afternoon when I was 11, to my following him down the cliff to High Cove. At sea level we wandered in our separate enchantments in and out of the rocky caves, over the sharp slate reefs which they say were once navigated by smugglers concealing their contraband at this hidden side of the island. We understood about tides up to a point – we knew that high tide filled the caves with water and that exploring them was for low tide only – but we hadn't yet understood how quickly the tide turned, how little time it took for the water level to rise. Preoccupied in the quiet space beyond the rocks, we turned back to the shore and found ourselves completely cut off from our route back up the cliff.

High Cove is the wildest part of the island, the furthest from dwellings or activity, too far for a shout to carry. Mobile phones didn't exist in the early eighties – even Patrick, the early adopter, didn't have his first Japanese brick until the end of the decade – and passing boats are sporadic. Even if we could have raised an alarm, what help, in any case, could we have expected? A fishing boat couldn't get in close enough, and what could have been done by a rescuer scrambling down the cliff to join us?

Marooned, alone, John and I assessed the distance to the shore. This was not simply a paddle; somehow the water between us and the rocks from which we would need to climb back up to the island proper was waist deep, chest deep, swimming depth. We had all swum fair distances around the island; we had swum triumphantly from Gull Island to Landing Beach, but here we were fully clothed, complete with wellington boots. Even Ross kicked his boots off on his pilgrimage to the island, but it didn't occur to us simply to abandon ours: we had not been brought up to that kind of profligate waste.

'Wild swimming' had not yet been invented, but John swam anywhere, then as now: in rivers, tarns, seas; in the rain, in the winter, in the nude. Faced with the requirement to get ourselves, our clothes and our wellingtons safely across the short stretch of water ahead of us, an elegant solution occurred to him. To swim in clothes would be difficult, to swim in boots downright dangerous, but lateral thinking transformed the problem boots into waterproof receptacles, and so we undressed and stuffed our clothes into our wellies. With one hand clutching a boot, held awkwardly out of the water so that the top stayed dry and our clothes were not swamped, we swam to the foot of the cliff. Leaving the first boot, we doubled back for the second. 'If not duffers, won't drown,' we concluded, triumphant, and climbed the cliff to rejoin our mother and Paul, sparing in the details of our afternoon activities.

On this trip, although he still swims daily, John's attention is on more domesticated water, spending days with mattock and spade digging out the final part of our plumbing system, the reed bed. Dave laid the pipe for grey water from washing up, washing machine, shower and basin to flow down into the topmost of the four tanks, filtering through the next three with their beds of cleansing reeds before it reaches the lawn below. This is the one flat space on the island, the 'croquet lawn', as Babs used to tell visitors: 'Of course, we've never had time to play croquet!' Jon is enthusiastic about this miniature wetland: he will plant willows, he says, to drink up the water trickling down. Before the tanks are installed, we are constantly emptying cans of washing-up water, five gallons at a time; the idea of grey water simply flowing harmlessly away is a luxurious one.

Finbarr is arrested in the doorway, on his first morning, by the sight of John, wearing only walking boots, standing in a large hole in the ground and swinging a mattock.

'Why is he nudey?' he asks.

'He didn't want to get his clothes dirty,' Sylvia explains.

There *is* a practicality in shedding clothes for these filthy jobs, and John generously takes on the worst. He is always clothed when he thinks other people are around, and we only ever hear one complaint: 'It wasn't a complaint exactly,' says Jon the warden, phoning me as I wait with Patrick for a hospital appointment in London, with John and Sylvia caretaking the house, 'more of a comment. One of our visitors said, "We saw a naked man with a scythe in the pouring rain – is that normal?"' Very wise, we thought, not to get his clothes wet: drying them in damp weather is not straightforward.

At the other end of the kitchen plumbing, there are four taps now on the sink: filtered rainwater – hot if the Esse is lit or the sun shining; unfiltered rainwater – though this runs out regularly over the summer, when the barrel to which it's connected empties; unfiltered spring water, for boiling; and filtered spring water, for drinking. John is as familiar with these as with the reed bed: he wakes early, swims from the beach regardless of weather conditions, and then comes to the house to make coffee and tackle the endless washing up which results from cooking every meal from scratch, with nowhere to buy a sandwich or a takeaway. He insists that the 'simple physical labour', both indoors and out, is a release after a long academic year of furious intellectual work, and of course I am too grateful to put up more than a token argument.

They must remember the visit as a time of labour – the digging and sawing, hauling damp logs from the wood and burning brash, tearing out ivy and lifting potatoes – but although I know this is true, in my memory our time together is one long, hazy picnic, drinking Pimm's and watching for dolphins from the lawn. We haven't spent so much time together since our childhood holidays twenty years ago and more, and this has the same tint of contentment: a break from the demands and dramas of our lives.

Felix, who crafted a replacement for half a rotten staircase in the Looe cottage, measured up Island House's rotten windows the Christmas before we moved in. He appeared to have neither camera, tape measure nor notebook, but we have faith in him; he inspires confidence: some kind of magic will happen.

Three months later, Darren, Felix's son, sits silent in the boat alongside his workmate Lee in a grey March dawn, holding on to the lovely, costly windows as the boat bucks in the open sea. Whose fault will it be if they break? he wonders. It is barely light: they've travelled an hour, loaded vast sash windows, heavy hunks of timber and glass, on to this slight boat, and have left the land, left the river, left the pier behind them to set out on the growling water into emptiness.

We watch them from the jetty, the sea as rough ('lumpy,' says Ernie) as the day Mick the gasman came out and almost failed to get home again, and wonder if we should have delayed the window replacement. They have several days ahead of them, of crossing at unsociable hours to fit in with the tides, and the wind is in the east. ('Nothing good ever came out of the east,' Ernie says, and begins a discourse on Stalin's Russia.)

In certain conditions, the wind and tide and current conspire to create 'runs' on the jetty: you feel a wave swelling behind you, and brace yourself for it to lift the boat, which Ernie holds as best he can with the engine, before it rolls away in front to crash on the beach. The backwash tears back towards you and the boat pitches helplessly as the old wave meets the new one. For the sake of the boat, never mind your nerves, the aim is to make any landing in these conditions as speedy as possible: if you are nimble, and unladen, you can hop from the bench seat at the side of the boat straight on to the jetty, and be away without even pausing to hold it there, but the windows are both heavy and fragile. I always feel for the non-seafarers, trying to negotiate unfamiliar ropes and cleats in a volatile sea, and the window boys come from St Blazey way.

'Throw him the rope!' Ernie shouts to Darren, and Patrick reaches for it to wrap it around one of the wooden posts which rear up from the edge of the jetty, to stabilise the boat. Lee, eager to get out of this alarming limbo, starts to lift a window and Ernie yells, 'Not yet!' He is fighting to get another rope around a post further along, and as soon as the boat is held at both ends, he shouts, 'Now!'

Balanced precariously between the need for urgency and the need to take great care with the big sheets of glass, we manage to manoeuvre perhaps half the windows – two bedrooms, bathroom, kitchen and sitting room and hall – from boat to jetty, the boys on the boat heaving them up and across to us, before the wooden post at the prow end suddenly leans, groans, and breaks clean away like a dead tree snapping in a storm. We are aghast: have we really broken it? It has been there forever, as far as I am concerned – what on earth are the Trust going to say?

Ernie decides he has risked *Pania* enough. The way in to tie up alongside the jetty is narrow, a reef of rock close on the other side, and the sea is mightier even than Ernie's skill. He puts off, back out to sea, and Lee waves to us: 'Short day!'

I allow myself a quiet but anguished howl. 'They can't just go!'

Patrick is practical – 'He'll probably try the beach' – so we hammer up the steps from the jetty, through the little gate Babs put there to stop the dogs running down to the sea, up to the main path and then down the slope to Landing Beach. It is a familiar run, because the Atkinses had no means of communicating with a boatman in transit, and we were often wrong-footed by the boat landing at the beach when we were expecting the jetty, or vice versa.

They have indeed landed at the beach. It is a longer, more awkward reach to pass stuff from the boat down to someone in the water, but between the four of us, Ernie holding the boat as still as he can with a wooden paddle like a long oar, blade to the seabed, we unload the remainder. Relieved of her obligations, *Pania* sets off back to the mainland, and the boys look a little forsaken.

Our faith in Felix is rewarded: somehow the new windows are perfect replicas, identical in every way to the old ones but sound, newly painted, double-glazed. Replacing them is perhaps the biggest single job of the whole renovation, but the best bit is before they go in. Room by room, the rotten frames, cracked glass, bits of board where the glass has collapsed entirely, are taken out, and one by one each room is overwhelmed with light. They seem enormous, edgeless, and full of the sound of the sea and the frisk of the early-summer wind. It is a loss to fill them in again.

It is a revelation, too, to see the flesh and bones of the house beneath the skin of stucco and white paint. There is horsehair in the peeling plaster and lath below it, and in the big oblong windows in the east wall Darren finds two clay pipes, the stem of one of them engraved with a tiny face: a signature from the original joiners. You realise how organically the house has grown from the place: the expedient muddle of brick, stone and beach-sand concrete, pilfered and repurposed from other island buildings, from the fabric of the island itself.

Chapter 10

Self-Sufficiency

---

a couple of hundredweight of shove and jostle,
friendly but rough. Their loose mouths and twitching snouts
muddy my legs with kisses.

Chris Considine, *Pig-sitting on the island*

Walking up from the beach has always been a blur of flowers. There is wood and metal and stone, and words on signposts signalling the current owner's intent; there are plateaus of sea and grass and sky, and the sober greens of the sycamore, but the place is littered with flowers. There is pink-trumpeted escallonia ('A nice name for a daughter,' my mother suggested to me as a young adult. 'You could have twins: Escallonia and Begonia'), near the bottom of the path, and then scarlet fuchsia, with small, unshowy flowers. There are wild roses in the hedges, and tame ones rampaging over the walls of Smugglers Cottage – the yellow 'Golden Wedding' which Babs bought Gus and Sheila when they'd been married fifty years. All along the path are the white, fragile flowers of the bullying brambles. There are flowering purple hedges of hebe everywhere, and, along the ancient wall between the house and Jetty Cottage, a spectacular row of hydrangeas, blue, pink and white. Near the house, Babs used to have an old boat stuffed with flowers, sweet peas scrambling up the rigging, and Claire has a big pot of sweet peas there too in the summer, opposite the honeysuckle which covers a wall of the house, behind a pot of foxgloves. Around their vegetable patch, she grows marigolds, nasturtiums, love-in-a-mist.

In the spring, there are thousands of violets along the path, and Sheila has planted snowdrops, crocuses and snake's head fritillary opposite the old daffodil fields, which flower patchily now; there is one half-field still strong with white 'Beersheba' daffodils, a pale blaze early in the year. Babs used to give me cuttings or seeds: weigela, in several healthy fragments, which I quickly killed; shaggy pink opium poppies, which grew gladly in gardens in Yorkshire and London.

I dream of flowers. I buy cheap and expensive plants – lilac, Christmas roses, peonies – and keep them in pots until the half-round flower bed under the sitting-room window is safe from builders' trampling feet. Then I fill the bed with delphiniums and lupins, Californian poppies and sunflowers, and almost everything fails. The trembling plants are doomed by my relentless optimism, by the gleeful snails, and most of all by the wind, careering in from the south-east with salt in its mouth to burn and wither almost everything I plant.

I tell myself that flowers must be a low priority for the pragmatic countrymen we aspire to be: we want food. With Jon, we tour our patch of land, which slopes up from behind the house to a point at the edge of the woods, bordered on one side by the stock fence which keeps the Hebridean sheep on the west side of the island, and on the other by what were Babs and Attie's vegetable gardens and are now, better kept, Jon and Claire's. The land above the house is bisected by a path, which runs parallel to the house and forms part of the visitors' self-guided walk – until at the end of the season Jon is prompted (although he is too polite to say so) by our litter of broken machinery, chunks of wood, forgotten tools and unkempt beds to reroute the trail.

Below the path, towards the house, are half a dozen venerable apple trees and the sisters' washing line; above it, a second path curves away into the wood, and is planted on one side with some of Jon's young native trees: field maple and hawthorn, hazel and willow. It must be hard for him to walk away from our patch of land, with those trees and the thriving patch of wild flowers, as it must be to have close neighbours; to have the island population increased by 50 per cent, and by people who are nostalgic, sometimes, for the old days before the Trust took over. He and Claire have a clear vision for the place, and passionate priorities, and we respect those and their knowledge and experience. We promise to keep cutting the grass in the wilder spaces until May or June, and then leave it for the flowers; not to work on the pond till the autumn; to prune the apple trees in late winter; to plant trees with a view to the long term, and their size and shade.

Most of our land is taller than I am with a wildness of bramble and ivy: hawthorn and tamarisk and oak are hardly surviving under the violence, and the rotavator we've been lent is dead.

'I was thinking,' I suggest to Jon, 'I could put my vegetable patch over there, perhaps?'

We look at the patch of thinner brambles which runs along the stock fence.

'I wouldn't,' he grimaces, 'too exposed. I'd go in here.'

The three of us turn to look at the area above the main path, perhaps forty feet wide and who can say how deep. It appears absolutely solid, an eight-foot-high rampant jungle with bramble as its skeleton and armour.

'Bloody hell!' I am appalled. 'Really?'

Jon fetches his Turkish scythe and takes a few pulls, slashing cleanly through the trunks. The welter of weeds is not quite as packed as it seems, at the base.

'Take you three or four days, with the slasher,' he tells me.

'It might take you three or four days!'

'I could probably do it in a day, to be honest,' he replies, modestly.

What I really want to do, fired up by the River Cottage *Pig in a Day* DVD, is to get a couple of pigs in to do the work for us, but this is vetoed by both men.

'Next year,' Patrick promises.

Next year, part of the vegetable patch is more or less up and running, but much of our land is still bramble and scrub, and I keep Patrick to his promise. We research breeds by eating all the rare-breed bacon we can buy, and arrange to buy two British Lop pigs: placid, long-snouted, and extremely tasty.

We plan carefully for their advent. The 'Practical Pig-Keeping' course I take includes a riotous afternoon loading weaners calmly into a trailer. We haven't, of course, got a trailer, and if we had pigs in one they could only get as far as the quayside, but we have cunningly circumvented this issue by buying the biggest dog crate we could find. This will go in the back of the car, and then be lifted – calmly – into the boat, and off on to the jetty at the other end.

'It doesn't fit,' says Patrick, as we set up ashore for the pig collection.

'Of course it fits,' I growl. 'We measured it.'

We wrestle and wriggle some more.

'We're going to be late,' I tell him, and Patrick snaps:

'I KNOW we're going to be late!'

We pause for a moment, trying not to lose our tempers.

'It's the height,' he says. This has become clear: we measured the length and width of both crate and car, but the roof of our boot is low and slopes lower, and we failed to consider the height.

'And we haven't got the holding number, have we?' he adds, quite unnecessarily in my view. I have sent off for this crucial piece of red tape, which identifies our property on the animal-movement form: the processes are strict, with foot and mouth and other calamities a recent memory. But postal deliveries are haphazard; we might have a sackful of post once a fortnight, and at present that sackful is sitting either in the sorting office or, perhaps, the harbour office: it is the weekend, and both are shut and locked.

Two young Lops and their owner are waiting for us just over the border in Devon, and we can't postpone. We step away from the brewing argument; we'll recalibrate, be flexible, find another way. We will put the pigs loose in the boot, with a straw-covered tarpaulin under them, then decant them into the crate in the mouth of the cottage's courtyard; we'll borrow the Trust's holding number for now and then make another official move once we get our letter from DEFRA. What can possibly go wrong?

The pigs are terribly sick on the way home, which is a smell we never quite lose from the car, but they don't storm the front, and, with a Looe neighbour's help, the transfer to the dog crate is surprisingly successful. The crate, however, with two well-grown weaners and no centre of gravity as they shift uneasily about, is too heavy to carry. Patrick and I stagger around in the middle of the road, collecting an appreciative audience, who eventually take pity on us and help to manhandle the crate down to the boat. Ernie is delighted by his celebrity cargo, and gets on the phone.

'I've got the pigs aboard!' he yells to his daughter. 'Bring the boys down!'

Ernie's grandsons are around two and four years old, and we can cope with their interest, but the boat is thronged with talk and photography from the quayside and we're almost as relieved as the pigs when Ernie unties her and we head out to sea. They immediately perk up in the sea air, grunting appreciatively and sniffing the salt. Sausage and Bacon are finding their sea legs, and moving rapidly to their new home.

We learn, as they sniff the brambles the next morning, that even thick-skinned pigs have reservations about being scratched all over; they are happy to trample fallen foliage into submission, but the snoutiest pig is put off by an impenetrable thicket of thorns. We end up preparing the way with the Turkish scythe, and then it's true that there is nothing like a pig for rotavating. As agricultural tools, they are an unqualified success, fertilising as they go, but understanding them as food is more difficult.

We thought that the names would help; we thought it would help to admire the size of their growing hams every time we saw them. But we underestimated the dog-like charm of pigs, the way they quickly learn to roll over when their backs are scratched, and grunt and stretch with pleasure, willing you to continue well after your arm is tired. When we try to move them from one well-dug area of the garden to another, they flatly refuse to step over the now invisible line where the electric fence used to be. Eventually, the lure of the food we're proffering is too strong to resist, but something spooks them when they do cross the line, and they set off at a gallop over the vegetable patch. After two hours of pursuit, enticements and attempts to outwit them, we manage to persuade them into their new pen. Our friend Martin (now regretting staying on pig-moving day) has very nearly collapsed with a heart attack, and we have gained a new respect for the independence of mind of a pig.

We simply fail not to get fond of them. When Bacon, the smaller and sweeter pig, gets mild sunstroke, I find myself sitting beside him in the shade, covering him with wet towels and stroking his hot head. Any farmer would despise me.

But when Sausage demonstrably hits puberty, the moment of dispatch can't be put off much longer. My stepsister Lucy, now around twenty years old, is staying on the day we've arranged to kill our pigs; she wakes at the early hour of death and sits heroically with me in the kitchen, listening to the shots.

Patrick comes in to tell me he's heading off to the butcher's with the carcasses and to leave the clearing up for him. 'Don't go out there,' he tells me, grimly.

Lucy, no less of an animal lover than I am, and still, in my eyes, pretty much a child, volunteers to go out and deal with the blood. This is her first proper visit to the island, apart from our wedding day; she wasn't born until I was 18, and so there's never been a good opportunity to bring her; she was only 12 years old when Babs died, and visiting became more complex. This is not quite the introduction to the place I would have designed, but her unflustered embrace of the general mess, the endless painting to be done, and the blood in the garden, makes me fonder of her than ever.

I can't leave the blood to her, however, so I ask her to put the kettle on instead while I head out and cover the worst of it, shining and glutinous, with beach sand we brought up for mixing concrete. In fact, although the whole experience nearly turns me vegan ('But what would you eat?' reasons Patrick, given that I don't in fact eat vegetables), the pigs' death seems about as good as a death can be. 'Surely they realise?' I agonised to the experienced friend who helped and advised us with this and subsequent pig-killing. 'Surely when you shoot the first one, the other one thinks – what the hell?' He looked at me pityingly. 'They don't think like us,' he said, and although I'm ashamed to say that I've never yet been present at a pig-killing, Patrick assures me that they really don't. The pigs get their breakfast; one of them is shot; the other keeps eating with total unconcern until the marksman finds his new target and the next pig follows the first. It doesn't seem like a bad way to go: you're alive, you're dead, without knowing anything about it. How many of us would choose that over most human deaths?

We never get used to it, though. We have many pigs over the years, and they all have happy lives and easy deaths, but our increasing conviction that 'happy meat', treated with respect and care in life and death, is not a bad thing can't quite square the grotesqueness of eating something whose tummy you've scratched.

We don't plan to have birds for meat, but in the interests of increasing our egg supply, we get a couple of Abacot Rangers – a good breed for laying – from Tina in the harbour office. The female is particularly pretty, white flecked with black, with the shadow of a light brown hood, but she comes with a green-billed husband who is more enthusiastic than we expect about his new harem, leaving them limping and bald about the back of the neck. Mainland predators mean that ducks there are always shut away at night, but we have no predators here and our ducks prefer to make their own nests – but mainland ducks lay indoors at night, and their eggs are collected before any fertilised ones have a chance to develop. Our ducks take themselves off in the spring, and we take their eggs when we find the nests. I usually leave a few, though, and do so without thinking for the Indian Runner whose nest I find with a dozen eggs tucked in with grass and down.

A week or so later, there is a great deal of quacking around our pond. The mallards sometimes bring their broods to the pond for their first swim, so I half expect to find ducklings there. The mother who is instructing the six ducklings on the water – three black, three yellow – is not a mallard, however; she is the maternal Runner.

It's impossible not to like them. 'He looks just like his mother,' says Patrick, proudly, watching them on the lawn a couple of weeks later. They are ridiculously sweet, all noticeably upright, like their mother, from the first; the three yellow babies are now striped. Their first weeks are in blazing, cloudless June, and we pity the poor mother, constantly on duty. The ducklings have swimming lessons, insect-eating lessons, garden-exploring lessons, and become rapidly more independent. The older ducks have no patience with the ducklings and peck them out of the way on the pond if there is an appealing insect at stake. We buy 'chick crumb', in which they show little interest; we laugh when the boldest bustles out with the rest of the ducks at feeding time, with no idea, at a week old, what he is quacking for.

The next day, one of the striped ducklings turns up to compete at breakfast time, but by mid morning we find him motionless and perfect in the spot where we scatter the food. I pick him up, insubstantial as a dandelion clock in my hand, and cry, ridiculously, as I bury him under the hebe. We institute supervised feeding: the mother duck has been astonishingly successful at hatching all six of the eggs left to her and keeping them alive for a full week; the survival rate of the wild mallard ducklings is pretty low. Our ducks are protected by their proximity to humans, which largely removes the threat from black-backed gulls: the pitiless pirates of the island.

Ultimately, though, humans are the great predator. A couple of the ducklings are drakes, and farmers the world over know that too many males are undesirable. We can't afford to feed nine ducks, none of whom are currently laying; we can't cope with more fertilised eggs hatching secretly in the undergrowth to survive, miraculously, into adulthood. The female ducks can't cope with the demands of even one drake; we have had a female lame for weeks now, crippled by the aggressive sexual tendencies of the male who pecks the necks of his concubines bald.

We advertise in the local smallholders' newsletter, in the local farm supplies shop and online; we offer the drakes to friends, acquaintances, the vet. No one wants them. 'You're too soft!' Ernie keeps telling me, when I confess I don't want to kill them; but we are trying to toughen up. The night before a friend comes to help us dispatch the pigs, we separate the ducks into two spaces: the damned and the saved. We think it will be all right in the morning, when we have suitable expertise on hand, but in fact there is a horror of flapping and trapping before the tools are wielded, the flapping becomes spasmodic, and ceases.

I find myself holding a slender black duck, retrieved from the mesh fence where escape attempts had caught him by his neck like the cormorants trapped by the illegal fishing net. We spent patient hours cutting them out, working for their survival, but this time the freeing is a deceit. I hold him for some minutes while his brother is killed, and I hold him again, warm and soft, when we start to pluck: heads in plastic bags to keep the blood contained, feathers and down ripping easily out of the skin.

Margaret, Ernie's wife, sits next to me and we pluck together as the others go off with the shot pigs; we talk comfortably in the sunshine of family and poultry until the tide runs out and she returns to shore. She and Ernie are country children, wartime children: they have always lived off the sea and the land, and the blood and feathers are nothing to them.

Patrick is equally bullish: he texts in the afternoon to say he is on his way back from preparing the carcasses of the pigs for butchery. 'I've brought you a special present,' he tells me, proudly. 'Do you like pigeon? The butcher gave me some. Feathers and all!'

At home, as I clean up blood and dismantle fences, the ducks remain silent. At five o'clock, when I rattle their feed bin, they come out to eat, but they say nothing.

The supplies from the vegetable patch which the pigs help to dig, and which the ducks clear of slugs, are a purer pleasure. For the first summer, we share Gus's little patch, near the main path down to the beach and either side of the superb globe artichoke: I do some of his digging, and he advises me on the sowing and care of peas, broad beans and lettuces, and provides twiggy support from the cherry plum tree in the Smugglers garden. As soon as we can, we plant our embryonic vegetable patch behind the house with potatoes, using Gus's patent methods to 'clear the land' – 'Of course,' he warns us, 'it's you doing all the work, with all that digging; the potatoes don't do it themselves!' – and at the end of the year, we have enough to keep the four of us for at least part of the winter. We plant cuttings of blackcurrants and raspberries, and optimistically sow rhubarb and asparagus seeds. We talk to Gus and Sheila about fruit trees, and plant a pear, a plum and an almond near the apple trees.

Although we grow, with varying degrees of success, a vast number of vegetables over the years – tomatoes, cucumbers, chillis and peppers in the greenhouse; onions and garlic, carrots, beetroot, parsnips and spinach; lettuces, radishes and salad leaves; sprouts and broccoli and cauliflower and kale; peas and sugar snaps, runner and broad beans, asparagus and sweetcorn – I never learn to eat them. Patrick, nibbling freshly picked peas, can't believe it – 'Try it, Moo, go on!' he urges me, and I do, but they taste just as they always have: impossible.

As the vegetables expand, we have endless bonfires to shift the piles and piles of debris: as well as bramble and dead escallonia, and the fuchsia which grows like a weed, we burn rotten window frames and broken shelves, cardboard and paper and corks. We make huge, loose piles which catch and blaze against all probability, and carefully packed constructions on which we expend match after match with only the most feeble of flames. I stand there as the day darkens, on duty with a garden fork, and cannot persuade myself to move away from the compelling, brilliant eye of the fire. There's a long-forgotten sensation to being outside as darkness falls; an echo of childhood, wondering exactly when it turns properly dark, knowing that if you go indoors when it's dimming, but quite light enough to play outside, the world can turn suddenly, shockingly to night once inside the house.

We burn what we can of what we strip out from the house, and two huge sacks of sawdust are destined for the fire. After four days of dogged, knee-bound work, Dave's mate the floor sander is considerably less jolly than when he arrived, and we are greatly relieved that we didn't follow our first impulse, to hire a sanding machine and do the job ourselves. The floors, dark and dulled with decades of dust, gleam a mellow gold; we can't stop looking at the staircase, which has always seemed unnecessarily imposing but now, with sun lighting it from three windows, is a gilded beauty, smooth and expansive.

'You need to be really careful,' Patrick tells me, when we have concluded that the bagfuls of sawdust are only fit, due to the chemicals in the ancient wood stain, for the bonfire. 'It's very flammable.'

'That's a good thing, isn't it?' I suggest, and nod blithely while he cautions me.

The sawdust goes on to a garden bonfire, which is already going pretty well. Heeding Patrick's warnings, I tip on quite a modest amount, and am immediately engulfed by flame. It glances at my face, then shoots over my head and down my back, and I don't know if I am on fire. Instantly, I lose any facility for rational thought or behaviour. I know quite well that the proper thing to do if one is on fire is to roll on the ground, but I simply can't bring myself to get closer to any possible flame. To roll on top of it seems so contrary to instinct that I don't: I run screaming down the grass from the vegetable patch to the shingle path to the house.

I know also that Patrick won't hear me. His hearing aids allow him to hear things close to him – in the same room, say – fairly well, though he is reliant on lip-reading too: his hearing is very limited. His parents were determined that he shouldn't be excluded from wider society, so years of speech therapy have resulted in speech which is almost perfect, and he avoided a 'special' school only by boarding at the one independent school which was prepared to take him. He is an exceptionally successful professional and businessman, and there is not much his hearing loss prevents him from doing; but coming to the assistance of his screaming, possibly flaming wife is one of those things.

I am gibbering after the thirty seconds it takes to reach him, and he has a lot of calming to do, though happily no flames to extinguish. I have lost most of my eyebrows and the front of my hair, and appear to have a vicious case of sunburn, but Patrick's administering of ice and chocolate gradually calms things down.

I think of my brother Paul, a volunteer fireman, in the bush fires of Australia, and then I do my best to put those thoughts aside.

Frightened by the reality of our interdependence, of our need for each other and the seriousness of the hearing loss which until now has been no more than an occasional inconvenience, I write an impassioned letter to Hearing Dogs for Deaf People. Patrick has been on their waiting list for five years, a timescale affected by the complexities of installing bomb-proof dog poo bins for a dog and its owner working at Canary Wharf; by the high failure rate the charity are finding in their policy of training rescue dogs;

and now by our move. But living here makes me uncomfortably aware of our vulnerability: if Patrick doesn't hear my cries for help, or if he is alone and doesn't hear an intruder, there is often no one else. Could we get another dog while we wait? I ask them; at least it would bark if something happened. They reply soothingly, explaining that you can't have a pet dog as well as a hearing dog, it would be too distracting, too confusing, but that Patrick is high on the list . . . So we wait, and worry, and my approach to bonfires becomes much more conservative.

Skipp is very polite when he arrives, a year later, but he carries his red and yellow soft toy, Dougal, everywhere, for comfort. He soon has a box full of toys – a polar bear, a rabbit, several penguins, a couple of dogs. Whenever he feels anxious, which is still quite often, he feels safer holding on to a toy, a ball or a stick. We are convinced he has abandonment issues. Hearing Dogs train their dogs jaw-droppingly well, and kindly, but the system involves some painful separations for everyone. A weaned puppy goes to the home of one of an army of puppy socialisers, who bring the young dogs up for about a year and whose hearts break when the dog goes off for its intensive few months at one of the training centres. The young dogs live in kennels for most of this time, though they also have 'bed and breakfast' accommodation for weekends out with new families, and bond now with their trainer. With five years of an old-fashioned boarding school behind him, exeat weekends spent with his friend Martin,

Patrick sympathises. By the time Skipp arrives with us, we anthropomorphise that he is determined not to lose another companion; certainly now, if Patrick leaves him, or we do anything which might mean we're going off the island – cleaning, for example, or packing bags – he goes into a steep emotional decline, and keeps Penguin or Sausage Donkey firmly in his teeth until the crisis is over.

Darren, the trainer who conducts our follow-up visits once Patrick has taken delivery of Skipp, will have none of this nonsense. As a youth, he worked with gundogs, and his time with army dogs was to balance the intensity of his main role as a sniper. He is brilliant and unsentimental, teaches us how to make cider and how to stop Skipp from getting 'too big for his boots', and he has no truck with soft toys.

But Skipp has a soft heart and a clownish grin, and it's a challenge for us to be tough with him. He has the greed of a Labrador and is paid in food – a piece of biscuit every time he alerts Patrick to a sound; sometimes he makes sounds up, or alerts him to music on the television, in the hope of picking up extras, but he is too transparent to pull it off. 'What is it?' asks Patrick, and Skipp should lead him to the sound or, if it's a fire alarm, lie down so as not to lead him into danger. After a false poke, you can see his brain whirring: what can I make up? 'It's nothing, is it?' Patrick asks him, several times a day, and Skipp grins.

The resistance to having another dog on the island is not quite as violent as with the cats, though we keep him on a lead for a year.

He's impeccably trained by the charity, though, ignoring pheasants whirring up under his nose, walking stolidly to heel past the sheep, who are fascinated by him and follow him on many of our walks, playing grandmother's footsteps so that they are all motionless, a few yards behind, when you turn to see if they're still there on their quiet hooves. To Patrick, he's a revelation. Alarm clocks, whistling kettles – the only sort we have – telephones, and the crucial smoke alarm are all now accessible to him through his dog, and I no longer worry about leaving him alone on the island, thinking of him sleeping with his hearing aids out, vulnerable to every sort of disaster. Ashore, daily interactions have Patrick's deafness signposted by Skipp's working coat, and the world seems a far kinder place to him now that people in shops and cafés and the street make an effort to speak so he can hear them, and don't write off a non-response as surliness.

In the winter, when human contact shrinks to each other, the storms are relentless and we are always cold, Skipp wakes up happy every day and greets us with an offering from the toy box, and we can't stop ourselves smiling.

Chapter 11

Into the Winter

———

The watcher on the beach
sees no horizon,
only a luminous blur where blue-grey
meets blue-grey, colour of distances.

Chris Considine, *The Secret Island*

It is September, and everything is now 'the last before winter': the last guests; the last visit from the builders; the last major delivery. The window for activity is shrinking as the autumn wind rises.

Patrick's father, Vernon, and his stepmother, Penny, who have been such stalwart workers over the year – decorating, ground-clearing, woodworking, gardening – are the last visitors. They are painting, at speed, yet more of the inside of the house; they have already addressed the kitchen and sitting room, and now they are painting the insides of cupboards, the neglected walls of the pantry, ready for the last great event of the season: our furniture delivery.

Graham, boss of the Cornish removal company who have had our belongings in storage since we left London nearly a year ago, is breezy about the serious task of transporting a houseful of furniture across the sea in an open boat, and thence up a few hundred yards of shingle path, by hand. He is wisely prepared, with half a dozen men. The weather is more of a concern, and with gales of Force 5–7 forecast and the sea freshening, Patrick is lucky to make it ashore to meet the removal men as planned. They move fast, making light of the back-breaking process of shuttling furniture from the van and the cottage on to the boat, off the boat on to the beach, and up the narrow path to the house. It is a huge help being able to use *Islander* again, back from the overhaul of her engine at Rock and ready for work: handing sofas and dining tables over the side of *Pania* would be almost impossibly awkward, but the removal men can simply walk on and off along the *Islander*'s ramp, nonchalant under large pieces of furniture.

As the tide turns, most of the men are aboard *Islander* or handling things ashore, with just one of them, back from carrying a huge armchair up to the house on his back, now waiting on the beach with me, watching the orange boat ploughing the sea towards us. There are only a couple of loads left to go, and Graham and the others are within shouting distance with another boatful when the boat stalls.

Patrick gazes at the engine as Tim the boatman tries to diagnose the problem: the gearbox? The jets? The boat has not long been in the water since its troubles of the spring, but her trip to the north coast for costly and lengthy fettling in specialist hands has not given her the new vigour and steadiness that Tim might have hoped for.

She drifts westward, towards one of the glass-bottomed boats which take groups of people round the island: excitements in the water under the glass bottom may not quite be those of the Great Barrier Reef, but viewing the island and its caves and seals from the sea has its own charm. This group have a shipwreck to enjoy, or at least the rescue of a becalmed vessel. Tim is forced to accept a tow from them to stop the *Islander* from drifting out to sea or into rocks.

For the two of us on the beach, it's impossible to see what's happening: we have no idea what they're playing at. Why have they stopped the engines? Why are they messing about chatting to the glass-bottomed skipper? The tide is cutting and time is running out.

When we see the lifeboat, we understand. Over a 12-month period, the lifeboat is called out around half a dozen times for the *Islander*, which is serious both for the lifeboat crew and the cost implications of a call-out, and for the pride of the skipper – not to mention the island's income and, now, the safe delivery of our household fittings.

The stranded removal man is invited to board the lifeboat,

which he does with great alacrity. *Islander* is ignominiously towed into the harbour, and the contents deposited in Bassett Court, which is quickly entirely full, with cupboards stacked on top of the piano and piles of tables towering to the ceiling. Unpacking boxes on the island, we think how little we've missed all this stuff, and are happy for the last bits in the cottage to come over slowly. I once read an article illustrated with photographs of families around the world standing outside their houses with all their belongings, the entire contents of the house around them, and I feel ashamed as I look at the lavish extent of our stuff and picture how it would look next to the possessions of some of those other families.

Very early the next morning, the bulk of the furniture and boxes stowed, we stand with Vernon and Penny on the beach. We've taken them for granted all year, on many visits to the island, saving us a fortune on decorators and supplying endless moral support, and it seems fitting that they're our final guests this year, overseeing this last punctuation mark of our move.

The four of us peer uselessly into the whiteness. I have spent many island hours watching for the boat, from lookout points all over the island, and even to poor eyesight it usually becomes visible not far out of the harbour, a dark dot across the horizontal plain of water, moving towards the mast which warns vessels off the rocks at Midmain. But in fog like this, we are cast off from clues and landmarks, divorced from the mainland except for the portentous groan of the foghorn from the Banjo Pier: Ernie is only feet away by the time we see him. Patrick has devised a combined light and foghorn device from a wooden whisky presentation box, a torch and a car horn, to guide him into the jetty in bad weather, although even the *Pania* has some of the superior navigational aids of larger modern vessels, and perhaps they are at least equally useful. The island also has a light buoy by the long rock reef of the Ranneys, to the south-east, although that does little to penetrate this invisibility: centuries ago, when the chapel was manned, it would have had a role 'in the tradition of lighthouses, possibly served by two or three monks who in times of tempest and sea-fog lit beacons and tolled bells to warn ships from running too close to the rocks' (*Looe: A History and Guide*, by W H Paynter).

Crossing in the fog, the world shrinks to the bright figures in the boat: out of time and space. Ernie tells us how the fishing boats used to anchor up, cutting the engines to silence, with one man listening at the prow for the foghorn until he could point to it, and they'd steer the boat following his arm. Now, Ernie is nonchalant in guiding us the mile to the harbour ('Fifty years' experience!') and we breakfast ourselves back to society in the corner café by the quay.

The fog has lifted when we return in the evening to another departure: winter is coming and our human resources are leaving like migrating birds. Matt is back with a couple of mates, but Dave has finished his stint: he holds his hands gleefully out to us as we pass so we can see his white palms. The builders have embarked on the last and most transformative task of the year: painting the salt-blasted, greying outside walls of the house for the first time in decades.

There is a festive air as the builders' final onslaught begins. The reed bed for our grey water is finished, with a great deal more sand, ready for the reeds themselves. Dozens of long boards, painted in the sisters' signature bright blue, replace the rotten fascia boards around the house; angle-grinding reveals a lovely bluish stone around some of the windows, and the top half of the gable end around our bedroom window glitters a shocking, brilliant white. We all spend a long, sunny evening in the garden, exclaiming at the beauty of the house, while the remaining builders barbecue an odd assortment of food, and we celebrate with an odd assortment of drinks.

But the weather changes again, and the rain is torrential enough to persuade even Matt indoors. We are dismayed that the rain follows him, trickling through the ceiling in the hall, flooding through the doorway of Patrick's office outside. We sweep the water into an inadequate drain, rescue flotsam, move bucketloads from overflowing butts, and the builders grimly go back out to the guttering. After the first spurt of optimism, their last fortnight with us becomes a struggle against weather, against the power tools struggling with our still unpredictable electrical supply, and against the house itself, the height of the gable ends, the obdurate walls and their cracks and dents and algae.

But by the time they leave, in what is definitely autumn, the worst of the work on the outside is done, the house is in good heart. We have power, water, habitable rooms. The first stage of the renovation, the impossible list which had to be dealt with this summer, is – astonishingly – complete.

We decide to have a house-warming party, before the winter sets in. Our old friends live upcountry, or abroad, but we invite everyone we know in and around Looe. We invite all the builders who have worked on the house, some of whom are slightly taken aback, and the accommodating removal men. We invite all the local boatmen we've had dealings with, everyone we've met on our irregular visits to the little church on the quay, and Mrs Hocking from Tidal Court, our favourite B&B. We invite Ruth Jennings, who was with the Atkins sisters during their first months on the island; when Sheila introduced us, it felt like meeting a celebrity, she is such a key character in Attie's books. We invite the curator of the local museum, and at her suggestion a local couple descended from the Finn and Hooper families, the free-traders who lived on the island a couple of centuries ago. We invite Jennie and her family, who used to live in 1 Bassett Court, Rob and his daughter Gina, who own and visit number 2, and Maria and Chris, who we've met through their holiday cottage business in Looe. We invite people from the harbour office and people from the Trust. We devise an enormously complex system of boats to ferry them all across, explaining the different times to our different visitors; we worry they haven't all grasped the importance of not missing their boat, as the next will be booked full.

The weather blows up and we flail about wildly putting everyone off.

We try again the following year, and exactly the same thing happens.

We give up party planning.

Instead, as our first autumn in the house gives way to winter, we use Gus and Sheila as an excuse for a small celebration at every opportunity. With Jon and Claire off on their winter jaunt, we have tea parties for Gus and Sheila's birthdays, helpfully spaced only a couple of days apart; we buy a pumpkin and have them round for soup and lantern-making at Halloween, then for sparklers and sausages on Bonfire Night.

Winter is quiet, after the chaos of visitors and builders, and we miss humanity. Gus and Sheila, and their rapidly growing puppy, provide company and diversion, and Patrick and I cope better than we might have expected with the inevitable dependence on each other. When we argue, I storm off to the bird hide or lie, on a fine day, in the springy grass halfway up the hill, just far enough away to make the point to myself. In general, with joint goals and constructive outlets for our energies, we argue less than we did in London, where traffic and crowds kept our blood pressure high.

Outside work becomes unappealing as the winds rise, but we

carry on with the painting and odd jobs inside, and the house begins to warm with the winter fires. Sheep and ducks force us outdoors: although Sheila is the sheep whisperer, we take it in approximate turns to count them every day while Jon's away, in case one has been separated, stuck or injured. They gather on inhospitable slopes to the west, beside High Cove, on Little Island or in the relative shelter of North Mead, and even with my poor eyesight I can easily count them. They tolerate us coming quite close, sober in their shades of brown and black and grey, all with neat black legs and heads, and impressive curving horns, quiet on the hillside. They look at me with interest, but neither follow me nor run away.

At Christmas, my mother joins us: we are tickled that our house, with its primitive conveniences, is marginally more luxurious than her isolated Yorkshire home, currently without water or telephone, or much in the way of heating oil. Coming at short notice as her services fail, she doesn't pack for the temperature we live in, and complains bitterly about the cold. Although we are still struggling with the Esse range's moods, and the house is rather cool, it is luxury compared to our ascetic stay in Jetty Cottage, and we are comfortable enough, we discover, with the temperature, with the gales, and with each other. We make Mother hot-water bottles, and stoke up the fires.

We are so delighted to have made it this far, to have achieved the wildly ambitious aim of making the house liveable within one summer season, to have it populated, after camping with an air mattress and two old armchairs all summer, with our furniture and belongings, that the winter seems easy. There are no visitors, of course; the business is not yet busy; the gales are not too severe, and the house keeps them, solidly, out. It is the first period of calm after the desolations of recent years and the excitements of the summer, and we breathe slowly.

There are five of us under the fairy lights for our first Christmas on the island, as well as dogs and cats. With Sheila in her Christmas jumper, and the Prosecco flowing, we smile at each other, my mother, our neighbours, our animals, as we toast our house.

Chapter 12

Animals and Insects

It has stood for weeks now. I thought it had stopped –
jar not quite full – but no, the bronze
level has crept up . . . Nothing's synthesised,
synthetic, changed by human hand

Chris Considine, *Thou watchest the*
last oozings, hours by hours

When our first spring comes, we settle into the good life, chipping away at painting the outside walls – the builders painted, tantalisingly, just the top half of one gable end before the weather stopped them – fine-tuning the electrical and water systems, scrubbing old slate floors and making endless small fixes to the house. Patrick and Justin's business is still in its infancy and money is tight, but we're not worried yet. We are content with each other, our house, our dog and cats, the sound of the gulls and the light on the water.

We wonder if we now count as smallholders, with our pigs,

ducks and vegetables. I study Babs's go-to gardening book, John Seymour's *Self-Sufficiency*, and we begin a four-year rotation of crops: potatoes followed by roots followed by legumes followed by brassicas; a space for soft fruit; beds for asparagus and rhubarb, growing astonishingly well from unpromising seed. The pigs slowly clear more land, and the boundary of the vegetable patch pushes slowly outwards. Patrick's family give us red- and blackcurrants, and I plant strawberries, raspberries and herbs. Gus shares the greenhouse we erect, humming as he tends his tomatoes. Seedlings outside are decimated by slugs, drought, pigeons, and crops are unpredictable, but the day we cut our first asparagus spear is a very proud one.

We talk about a cow for milking, so Patrick can make cheese, and we try to convince Jon of the merits of a few Exmoor ponies. 'I don't mind!' says Ernie, when we ask him if he'd have a cow on his boat. 'A small one,' we assure him, but the logistics of dealing with yearly calves seem insurmountable, even to our reckless minds.

Instead, we buy bees. 'Ah – you got them from Heather and Eddie,' the bee people of Cornwall validate us: these are bees of a good pedigree. On Patrick's birthday, I drive them home from north Cornwall, and slowly the car fills with them; the back windscreen is dark with buzzing. Eddie loaded them carefully in, with the hive strapped up, but they seem to be escaping; I wonder if there will be any left in the hive by the time I get to Looe. Further, while it's not as frightening as being on fire, being trapped in a box with an unpredictable cloud of potential pain is not a comfortable experience. I pause in a lay-by and phone Eddie for advice.

'It'll just be a few freeloaders, hanging on the outside,' he assures me. 'They'll stay in the back,' and they do.

Patrick, who has not accompanied me because we thought Skipp would not enjoy a bee-filled journey, thinks this is hilarious when I tell him. 'Freebees!' he chortles.

The bees are a birthday present for Patrick, who has ordered a bee suit as his present from my mother, but with our usual lack of planning, we have left the order slightly too late and don't yet have it in our hands. It is almost certainly in the harbour office, but the harbour office is closed at weekends, and today is Saturday.

Patrick meets me in Looe without the suit, and we unload the hive on to Ernie's boat and worry to Ernie about reassembling it without protection. He has just been fishing with one of his regulars, who turns out to be an angel.

'I keep bees!' he says. 'I've got a bee suit in the car – I'll just run and get it and then I'll come over with you and set the hive up.'

So it is that Mark crosses to the island with us, all of us rushing as the tide is on the way out. The bees are only reliably at home at certain times of day, so we haven't entirely been able to plan the expedition around the tides. Mark and Patrick dash about with the electric trolley (in a rare phase of compliance), the hive, Mark's box of bee equipment, our box of bee equipment, and Mark's all-important suit, until the hive is installed on its stand between the apple trees and the pond.

'They're very placid,' says Mark. 'Lovely bees. Very laid-back. Ah – you got them from Eddie and Heather . . .'

Mark continues to keep an eye on us, advising Patrick on feeding, treating for Varroa mite, extracting honey, lending us a 'super', which is like an extra storey, added because our bees are making so much honey. They remain very mellow for their first season, and only sting once, when Patrick tries to disassemble their house to show a visitor, without putting on the suit; later, interbreeding with the wild Cornish bees, they become more feisty. They line up in rows to go to sleep, and we like to show people the orderly lines of bees, gently moving as they snore the nights away.

As we only take possession of them quite late in the summer, we don't try to take honey in the first year, but by the following summer, Patrick simply can't wait. Mark has promised to come over with his equipment, crucially the 'spinner' for extracting honey from the comb, but Patrick opts for a more immediate, more hands-on approach. He lifts frames from the hive, removes the comb, and squeezes.

This is effective, in that liquid honey is produced. Some of it finds its way to the container Patrick has selected, and the rest soon coats the kitchen table, a number of spoons and knives, every chair in the kitchen and the fluffy cushion the cats like to sit on, as well as Patrick's bee suit and most of the floor. We end up with a couple of jars filled with honey laced with bits of beeswax and general grime, of which Patrick is enormously proud.

Thankfully, we are soon rescued by Mark, and process all the honey through the spinner: you add a frame of comb, frantically whirl a handle round, and watch the honey pouring out of a tap in the bottom of the container. It's then sieved through muslin into jars, dripping through slower and slower as time passes, to a deepening pool of beautiful, dark, clear honey. We get up to about twenty on our first harvest and are astonished by this 'something for nothing' magic; jam-making is satisfying, but you start with concrete ingredients which you've grown and nurtured, whereas honey comes from nowhere but the industry of the bees, and the soon-dead flowers of ivy, sycamore, apple.

We have proffered various home-made presents to our families since we've been here, with mixed success (the perpetually oozing Turkish Delight had to be thrown away; the ham had boar taint), but the first honey Christmas, we can finally be proud.

We are determined to get the ham right, though, and search every spring for rare-breed gilts, encouraged by our first foray with the Lops. Many farmers and smallholders don't yet seem to have a strong presence online, and we hunt for days to find a couple of weaners at the right time, and take whatever breed is available. We have Gloucester Old Spots, which make terrific sausages and are friendly characters: Onion, Mustard and especially Gravy, easily recognisable with her black ear. Like the Lops, they love being scratched and collapse within seconds into a grunting slab of pleasure. We have a couple of Tamworths, who have superb long snouts and glorious red hair, and who escape, as Tamworths do, whenever we go away.

'We were up at the fire pit,' Jon recounts, 'and my friend said, "Have you got wild boar here?"'

They're worth it, though, and enable us, finally, to make excellent ham.

The Large Blacks we try come from west Devon, not far over the border, and we decide to buy three. I turn up to South Yeo Farm East, from where we subsequently buy sensational beef and lamb, and lean over the side of the pen with Gillian, the farmer. There are our three pigs – all female. Despite widespread assurances that boar taint was semi-mythical and that weaners grown on for meat would be sausages before it could kick in, we were convinced that Sausage, the pubescent Lop, had it: the meat (especially that ham) had an indefinable quality, not quite gamey, not quite off, but definitely unpleasant. When I mention this to the butcher, he says he never touches anything but gilts, so from then on we stick with females.

Along with the three black pigs Gillian shows me is a fourth – about half the size of the others, the size perhaps of a dachshund. None of them are very big; it's been a terrible spring and the sow is evidently struggling to feed them, so they have been weaned relatively early. But this, Gillian explains, is the runt. The other weaners have all gone, but 'I don't know what I'm going to do with her,' she says.

'No,' I sympathise. 'It's a problem.'

'I suppose I'll just have to put her under a heat lamp for a bit and then – well, I don't know.'

'Mm, yes, that's tricky. Poor little thing.'

There's a pause, during which I gaze obtusely at the pigs, until Gillian says:

'Unless you'd like to take her? She might not survive, but – you can have her for free.'

It is irresistible. We have a grisly conversation about the legalities around disposing of a dead pig, in case she doesn't make it, and then we load all four of them into the second attempt at dog crates: three smallish ones, which are easier to handle and do actually fit into the car. The runt is so small that she fits in with one of her sisters, with room to spare.

They travel reasonably well, although landing them we have the only mishap of our career as animal transporters: Patrick trips getting off the boat with a crate of pig in his arms, and it falls into the water. Instantly rescued, the pig seems remarkably unmoved, resigned to this day of shocks in cars, boats and crates. This is the only spill in the process of transporting a total of two cats, three dogs (including both of Sheila's), five ducks, eleven pigs, and around thirty thousand bees, which we think is not bad going.

We get them up to the house without further incident, and think about keeping them warm, in this cold and windy March. We have six-by-three-foot pig arks, and our pigs are usually happy throughout their lives in a single one of these; as they get older and the days get warmer, they tend to make themselves beds outside. The Lops were particularly keen on this, and would drag around suitable branches and the like in order to make themselves a nest. These pigs, though, are so little, and the weather so miserable, that the ark will be pretty draughty around them, and instead we move the duck house into the new scrubby area designated for clearing by pigs. The ducks have spent their first winter in our garden and utterly scorned the house, which we built for them out of carefully cut marine ply; happily ducks, unlike chickens, only need a simple shelter, with no nest boxes or perches. They haven't yet set foot in it, so we lug it up to the pig area and stuff it with straw.

The four black pigs snuggle neatly into it, but as we feed them over the next couple of days, we see that the runt is very shivery, and seems slightly disorientated, struggling to find her food. We decide to bring her indoors; we put the gas fire on and fill a box with straw to go in front of it.

She lies quite quietly against my shoulder, after the initial protest at being picked up, but she won't settle in the box. I put her back on my shoulder, and sit with her through the afternoon, her small snout snuffling into my neck. She is heavier and more solid than my best friend's baby, which I was holding in just the same way a few weeks earlier, but the warmth and helplessness are the same. She falls asleep there, and I hold her until she stops shivering, at which point I offer her warm porridge, which she rejects, and then take her back to her sisters.

Sheila and I repeat this for a few afternoons, while the weather remains unseasonably harsh; and the runt survives. She never quite catches up with her sisters, but she grows to a decent size and goes to the butcher with the rest. Perhaps it is because there are four of them and they have a pack mentality, but they are never sociable in the same way the other pigs have been: they are suspicious or indignant if we try to scratch their backs, and the runt has less sentimentality than I do about her quiet afternoons indoors.

There is a solid pleasure in using animals to manage the land: the Trust's Hebridean, then Shetland sheep grazing down the scrub; the pigs rotavating our vegetable patch. It seems incredible that until a century ago, the island must have been completely landscaped by farming and by beasts like these, or the 'horse and two cows' the eighteenth-century visitor noted. The oldest photographs show grassland cropped short, and before the trees which now cover much of the land were established – not much earlier than those turn-of-the-century photographs – the place must have been almost unrecognisable.

Beyond the sheep, introduced specifically for conservation grazing, and the pigs when they are with us, there are no land mammals here at all now, other than humans and, if the roof of a cave can be called land, bats. The rats and rabbits have been eradicated; there are no mice or voles or shrews; no hedgehogs, foxes, badgers or deer, bar an intrepid swimmer perhaps once a decade. The mink which escaped from the farm up the coast, and caused Babs such concern for her dog, didn't choose to breed here, and there is no record of stoats, weasels, squirrels; the wild boar just an old wives' tale. There are no frogs or toads, either, no snakes or lizards – just a few newts one year which evidently stowed away in some plant purchases. It is so peculiar not to have any mammal or amphibian wildlife, so ironic in a nature reserve. It is not immediately apparent, this lack, but as you start to notice the absence, the place seems underpopulated: the birds are aloof companions.

We can be consoled, though, by a thriving population of that most comforting of aquatic mammals, the seal. When I was younger, there was only one seal who was anybody in Looe, and that was one-eyed Nelson, the greatest Looe celebrity of his time and even more widely popular now as a statue on Hannafore beach. In recent years, though, with more scientific and regular surveys, a whole colony of seals have been identified and named, and are monitored as regular visitors to the island. While I don't know them as individuals, partly because my eyesight is feeble, I am as delighted as anyone to see an inquisitive head pop up above the surface of the sea to inspect our comings and goings, and fascinated too by the extraordinary, other-worldly sound they make on a misty day, a soft ululation with a rise and fall like a small choir pretending, badly, to be ghosts. It is entirely captivating, this ethereal noise out of nowhere, and if I were a sailor in an unscientific age, I too would weave stories of singing from the rocks which it is impossible to resist.

Chapter 13

Help

She can glimpse the south shore across an abandoned room,
gaze from the doorway towards the line
where blue and blue meet, or where the lower grey
and upper dissolve together, and wish
the island could slip its moorings . . .

Chris Considine, *Endings*

A wild afternoon, in the June of that year, waves washing across the jetty, and Ernie and his grandson Jamie struggling to hold the boat. Skipp is skittering about in a confliction of anxieties: getting his paws wet, losing Patrick, losing his footing, missing Ernie's proffered Bonio; the rest of us have our minds on loading ourselves and our belongings into the boat and don't spot Skipp's decision to leap aboard just as a wave has lifted the boat away from the jetty. He slots neatly into the gap between boat and shore, and lands with an explosive splash; consternation has barely started, though, before Jamie reaches in and hoicks him out by the handle on his life jacket as though he were an errant bag of shopping. Jamie is a fixture on the lifeboat now, and consequently saves lives with nonchalance.

Gus and Sheila wave us off gamely, upright among the lapping water. Island-sitter Karen, who with her husband Malcolm is standing in for Jon and Claire this year and has agreed to feed the pigs, stands just above them on the steps. I am aching, as I sit down in the boat, from an intensive couple of days digging a new piece of ground to put potatoes in; happily, it turns out that our artist friend Sasha, who has been staying for the last few days, is as handy with a mattock as he is with a paintbrush. It is early summer, already absurdly late to plant potatoes, and it will be my last gardening for the year. I am off to hospital: although keyhole surgery means that the hysterectomy I am about to have will be less catastrophic than it would have been a generation ago, convalescence will still take a bit of time, and No Heavy Lifting will be allowed

We return a week later, into the hands of our friend Ruth, who's been house-sitting and redecorating some of the wetter parts of the house (the wall in the stairwell is on its third round now). She looks after us tenderly for 24 hours, exchanging confidences among the broad beans, before delivering us into the care of my brother John, who has changed his flights from Canada to come to England a week earlier than he'd planned, to help. He does everything, quite apart from his usual labours outdoors (stacking wood, clearing bulrushes) – he cooks and washes up, hangs out washing and feeds the pigs. When he leaves, Patrick grasps his hand.

'I was right on the edge,' he says, 'and I really don't know how we'd have coped without you.'

We are all taken aback by such failure of the stiff upper lip, but it's true that we hadn't reckoned on the calamity of having one of us entirely out of action. The business is anxiously balanced, now, between failure and success, and the days of wandering away from the office to involve himself in house works are over for Patrick. Worse, the initial surge in his fitness ('I've seen a change in you,' Ernie told him, with pride, at the end of our first year – two years ago now) has dissipated, and he is in constant pain.

His mother died without knowing what was wrong with her, after fifty years of being told to pull herself together, but the syndrome her children inherited affected her heart much more badly than theirs: for Patrick, the chief difficulty is with muscle pain and stamina. Like his deafness, this is something he has generally simply ignored. He doesn't do long walks, and when I once persuaded him into our local pool in London, he was unable to move for a week after swimming a length, but day to day he has simply ignored the low but constant levels of pain. Here, though, the requirement for physical strength is of a different magnitude.

For my part, the emotional impact of a hysterectomy has been less than I feared, but for the first few weeks, with Patrick below par as well, the physical implications are disastrous. Everything that comes on to the island – shopping, animal food, compost – is loaded and unloaded by hand from the boat, and I can't do any of it. I was in pain of course before the surgery – though the cause of both that and my failure to get pregnant has resisted diagnosis – but when deliveries dictated, I could lift and carry. So far, we have been sufficiently young, fit and determined to manage the physical demands of island life which previous occupants navigated by having staff, or volunteers. Determination is not, now, enough.

With John's help, and Ruth's, we get over this crisis. I heal, and both the business and Patrick's stress levels stabilise. Within months, though, he is in hospital himself for a week, for observation, to see if the London specialists can come up with anything new (not really); I'm also back for another operation; our strength is reduced. Our family and friends are widely dispersed, and in any case we can't be completely reliant on their help. The initial push is over, but the demands of island life continue: how should we best face them?

Finances are tight: although the business now has employees with proper salaries, its directors are still drawing very little. We decide, however, that we can and must stretch to employing an 'oddjobber' for a day a month. Alan is in his late sixties and asthmatic, but he turns his hand to almost anything: building a new shed for extra winter fuel; painting the stairwell, again;

strimming and slashing and burning. We look forward to his visits, and those of the old hands – my brothers, Katie, Kath, conditioned by the sisters into working for the island the moment they set foot here – with craven neediness.

My brothers coincide for another visit later the next summer, as John makes his annual trip to England in the long vacation from his university job, and Paul is en route from Melbourne to Edinburgh, where he is taking a job for two years. He has the restless, unsettled streak which runs through the wider family, and has arranged this improbably splendid job, which seems to consist of roaming the Hebrides inspecting fire stations, in the space of a few weeks, by Skype. His wife is stuck in Australia with two small children, waiting for her visa and arranging logistics, and I drive through the night to collect Paul from Heathrow and bring him to Cornwall. Looe is not a logical stop on his journey, but the rest of his family are gathered here: I have summoned my mother, and it is the fifth anniversary of my father's death. We have obtained a celebratory salmon, but most of us are too tired or fraught to enjoy it.

Fortunately, we have entertainment. For the past few days, the demarcated area of garden serving as a stage has been invaded at every rehearsal; every time the performer sits or crouches or kneels, a cat or dog sees an invitation and comes towards him, purring or wagging, to be stroked. The duck pen is only a few feet away; so far their interruptions have only been vocal, comments on particular lines perhaps, but he expects webbed feet to intrude at any time.

It is blazingly hot. He is a redhead, according to friends – a strawberry blond, he corrects them – and hates the sun. His favourite month is November. He is wearing a hat, but at present he is also wearing, as part of his costume, a duffel coat. He pulls it up, over his head, so that he appears headless, and passes a flat hand, palm downwards, over the top to reinforce the impression. He emerges scarlet and tousled.

'Do you think it's better without the envelope?' he asks.

The envelope represents the helmet of Omega, renegade Time Lord and anti-hero of *The Three Doctors*, a seventies classic. We are rehearsing Martin's one-man play, *The Pyramids of Margate*, destined for the Edinburgh Fringe and various venues thereafter; I travel to London for some of the rehearsals, but some of them happen here. Martin and I met, he likes to tell people, when he was showing the world his Bottom: I was a shy 18-year-old, assistant director of a university *Midsummer Night's Dream*, and after a dozen subsequent collaborations as actor and director, we have reunited for this project. Patrick has known Martin even longer than I have, since school: Martin introduced us, of course, read at our wedding, chased our pigs, and now works – after some wooing – for Patrick's business. His working days this week are at his employer's head office, and we rehearse in the evenings, at weekends, on the odd day off. We mark out the dimensions of the Edinburgh stage in the garden, the only place where there is enough space to do so, and Mart performs to Gus and Sheila, to Patrick, to me and Skipp, and eventually to my brothers and John's family.

The island is inherently theatrical; there are many stages, perfectly framed for performance, on beaches, rocks, the chapel site, the woods. Twenty years before, touring a student production of Shakespeare's *The Tempest* to outdoor spots around the country, I performed on the top lawn here: we were in Cornwall, and the play is set on an island; it was impossible to resist.

I also knew that Attie, the more romantic and literary of the sisters, used to say how much she'd love to hear an actor deliver the speech from *Henry V* which ends:

'Follow your spirit, and upon this charge

Cry, "God for Harry, England and St George!"'

I therefore primed one of my *Tempest* cast to learn the speech, and was pleased to bring Attie this small gift.

I failed, though, to make careful plans. I telephoned the sisters, who made appropriately pleased noises, booked a boat, and left it at that. I gave no serious thought to the subtleties of staging, so that we performed prosaically on the croquet lawn, wasting the wonderful possibilities of the island. Nor did I think about finding an audience – or, it turns out, about not annoying the production manager, who deliberately dawdled on his way down with one of the actors, missed the boat and the tide and spent the day in Looe.

I put on Sebastian's costume myself; some of the ambushed day visitors gathered uneasily at the side of the lawn, and the performance commenced.

This was towards the end of Attie's life, when she was more unpredictable and less social than she had been, but I never found out the cause of the argument which kept her and Babs inside for the entirety of the play. Their distant, angry voices punctuated the verse, and the stirring rendition of Henry's rousing exhortation to his troops bounced blankly off the white walls of the house. There was no applause.

Mart's one-man Doctor Who-centric *The Pyramids of Margate* has a much better reception, and now 13-year-old Nicholas is nearly sick laughing at some of the sillier lines. Martin is well prepared for the black-box theatre of Edinburgh by the blazing sun of his island rehearsals, and buoyed up by his reception here. We are nicely distracted from grief, pain and jet lag, and by the time Skipp has eaten a plateful of profiteroles, the grave mood has lifted.

Gus, like Martin, is uncomfortable in the summer heat, and then as summer turns to autumn, he suddenly finds he can't get his socks on. The morning begins quite as usual: he makes the tea, drinks it with Sheila in bed and then, unhurriedly, starts to dress. But when he sits on the bed and bends to put on his socks, he simply can't do it.

Sheila, who could have been a nurse, knows what is wrong

with him. Ernie and Tony are due with the post, and by the time they arrive she has called the doctor, and the air ambulance is on its way. Tony, who has almost never set foot on the island in forty years of working the boat, comes ashore to help Gus to the croquet lawn, the one flat place where the helicopter can land.

We are on the mainland when Sheila calls us. 'Gus has had a stroke,' she says, quite matter-of-factly. 'Could you come back and look after things here?' Patrick commandeers Dave, one of the seagoing boatmen, to take him across, and I am halfway to the hospital when Patrick rings to say Sheila can't travel in the helicopter so I come screeching back to collect her at the quay. Gus is in remarkably good spirits when we eventually see him at the hospital, but he can't do anything with his left hand.

He is in hospital for both their birthdays that year, two days apart in October; their son Nick gets to the island so that his mother is not alone on her eightieth and I deliver Gus a Polish sausage on my way home from a funeral. The family are worrying and conferring about what should happen next – there is a rehabilitation unit in Bodmin where Gus might go – but the hospital telephones ten days after he went in to say they're sending him home, now, and home he comes without a coat, to be repatriated and carried ashore from the boat by the lifeboat crew.

He is slower, after this, and a little wobblier, and after six months he has decided it's time to go home: back to their other house, perched on a clifftop on Cornwall's north coast with views to Lundy. They begin the long, slow process of packing up fifteen years of island life. They have been the nurturers for years, for four children, elderly parents, Babs: they have been the practical ones, running the island as Babs declined, with imagination and fortitude. They have also, always, been the adventurers, moving in middle age from generations of safety in the Midlands to an isolated 'project' house in north Cornwall; from the house they crafted for themselves there to the wild island, in their sixties. This is their first backward step, based on pragmatism rather than desire. They remind themselves how lovely their house at Yeolmouth is, how lucky they are, how good it will be to have their daughter in the converted barn next door.

But in their last weeks on the island, Sheila wakes, without volition, into every kind night, where the hours pass more slowly as she looks out at the dark sea.

Chapter 14

Children

Now on the borders of the pools children arrive,
exclaim, and play with delight,
and the air is full of the movement of seagulls' wings.

Chris Considine, *'In this moon landscape'*

Carissa, who's seven, has found an extraordinary thing: 'It's white, and sort of translucent – is it a jellyfish?' Elma, at three, likes stones, and spends hours on the beach sorting through them, moving them in and out of her bucket. Finbarr, falling hard out of a tree, says with nonchalant rebuke, 'I guess that wasn't such a good one for climbing, after all.' Rachel, nine, helps to gut her first fish; she makes faces and squeaks with disgust all the way through, but insists on cleaning every one. Nicholas takes over feeding the pigs every summer, and always gives the most and the best apples to the underpig. Holly, at four, cries when she has to leave.

These children play football with Skipp (who cheats), and

hunt for eggs in the undergrowth round the duck house. They skim stones and swim shrieking in the sea, and manage not to fall out of boats. They scratch the pigs' backs and make dens in the woods. They eat and sleep and run. They and the island know each other.

There have been children here before: not just holidaymakers, but the Atkins relations Tony used to take to school every day; other schoolchildren before the war; the expanding Vague family in the century before that. 'If the weather was closing in, I'd go up to the school and say, you'd better come now,' Tony tells us of his charges; I pass this on to Isla, daughter of Angus, who fishes with Ernie's son Philip in the winter, and her eyes gleam.

It is one of the Wildlife Trust's first questions: 'This is awkward,' they preamble when we have our initial meeting with the bosses about the house, 'but are you planning to have children?' No, we assure them, we can't; but as we settle, the business stabilises, the children of our friends and siblings play on the lawn and Tony tells his stories, we think again.

We approach the adoption and fostering arm of the council, and the first few people we speak to make interested noises. 'No, I can't see why that would be a problem,' they say. 'We have people in all sorts of remote places.' We talk to the council first about fostering, but we soon grasp the logistical difficulties. 'Social workers' diaries just don't have the flexibility,' says ours, regretfully, prevented from crossing by weather for the third time, and meeting us in Looe to let us down gently.

'There's no point, I suppose,' I ask tentatively, 'talking to the adoption people?'

But he is enthusiastic about this: there is no ongoing interaction with social workers' diaries after the early stages of a placement.

'And I think a lot of children would really benefit from being somewhere like the island – particularly younger children, who really just need a huge amount of one-to-one time.'

Early in our plans for a family, Patrick was positive about adoption: his mother was adopted, after all, and she grew up happy and sane. Later, some old friends of his grew increasingly gloomy on the subject of their adopted children, about whom their complaints became graver as the years went on – from 'not doing well at school' to 'in trouble for shoplifting' – and he became a little warier. As we discuss my meeting with the social worker, though, Patrick is positive. 'It might sound weird,' he tells me hesitantly, 'but it's partly because of Skipp – I now know how much I can love someone who isn't in my family.'

I don't pass this on to the social workers in case it does sound weird, but I might as well have.

A group of eager couples in a council-decorated room, and a lovely success story wheeled out to tell us about her adopted daughter. Information on a whiteboard, and the terrible magazine with photos of children waiting to be adopted. The same conversation after the meeting, with new social workers:

is our location a problem? This time the assurances are breezy. No problem.

We stand on the beach a month later watching the water, and the movement of the boat containing our allocated social worker. We've landed in worse conditions, we reassure each other. Ernie wouldn't have brought her out if he hadn't thought he could do it – he didn't even hum and ha. But even from a distance, everything about his passenger, from her woolly hat downwards, is horrified, and after a couple of passes towards the beach, Ernie signals that he's not going to try to land her. We can hear the shrill laughter of her relief as they head back towards the mainland.

The moment she lands there, she phones to say we can't be assessed.

After six months of decisions overturned and apologies offered by senior social workers; contradictions, obfuscations and applications to Data Protection; MP surgeries and ministerial correspondence, we have one meeting – an assessment for an assessment – with a social worker, who admits at the end of it, 'There's nothing that *automatically* rules you out,' but the council ultimately sticks with their boat-averse woman with the woolly hat. They are not prepared to assess us. We can't ascertain how far this is really due to our location ('Of course we'd move,' we assure them, 'if that was in the best interests of the child') or whether they just didn't like us.

Ernie remains disgusted on our behalf. 'It's pathetic!' he expostulates. 'All those children out there! It's ridiculous! You should fight it!' But we have both spent much of our lives fighting, one way or another, and eight years of struggling to have children was enough. If I had had the choice: live here, or live in suburbia with children, I would have chosen the latter without a second's hesitation, but those choices are not always ours to make.

They still play, these children, every summer, in the rock pools and the gardens, and cry, sometimes, when they leave, and we watch them laugh and grow and find extraordinary things at low tide, and we wave until they're out of sight as the boatman takes them ashore.

Chapter 15

Movement

Imagine the cool flow along head neck body
over and under wings.   And as they fly they cry out
is it from pleasure?   Look at that gull
lying on the wind   and laughing.

Chris Considine, *Herring gulls over Little Island*

The ground is moving. There is bedrock, scattered with boulders, where there used to be sand, and without the beach to hold them at bay, the waves tear into the soft cliff, cutting open layers of sand, stone, silt to be exposed like the side of a bombed-out house. Branches fall, trees are uprooted; the brick archway which framed the old water sump is torn in half. Great chunks of old concrete, speckled with beach sand, are flung about the shoreline, relics of solid human endeavour. Immoveable lumps of rusty iron, of mysterious design – pumps? winches? – are revealed and then covered again. The steps down to the jetty begin to list.

When Jon and Claire return from their winter trip, they

reroute paths, further from the cliff edges, and we wait for the old paths to fall. 'It looks as though someone's been round with a bulldozer, and just scraped all along the edge,' Claire says, as they walk round.

We survey the beaches for bodies, the summer suicide for whom the lifeboats searched in vain. We search for lost cargoes, ancient relics, treasure. We find plastic bottles, cans, rubber gloves; fishing net and rope and crab pots. Sometimes, parts of the Flying Fortress lost in the Second World War are washed on to the island; twice, a message in a bottle. One of them, from a student in Belgium, asks for and receives a reply; her father sent it into the sea for her, from his fishing boat. The other mourns a dead baby.

One winter, we have dead dolphins, or porpoises, washed up – four or five, gradually stripped by seabirds and water and returned as bones to the sea and the sand. My mother, collector of sheep and rabbit skulls from her moor in Yorkshire, boiling up anything with remaining skin or fur to clean bone, is pleased with the dolphin skull (scoured by the sea) which we give her for Christmas.

When I was a child, there was a year of conger eels; a hundred years ago, a whale. Gus and Sheila found the headless body of a spaniel, and buried it high on the beach, until the sea found the remains and took them back

Around the island, trees are split in half and hedges burned bare in the wind. We fix and fix the shed roof, the panes of glass in the greenhouse, and gather up escaped bins and buckets. The windows are covered with spray and the paint salt-blasted, but the house stands solid.

To be out in the storms is exhilarating, but sitting in the house with the wind relentless around us, we have to struggle to hold our nerve. 'It gets in amongst you,' my father would have said. When I was teaching, it explained a lot. 'Why are they all so wild today?' someone would complain in the staff room, and then we would realise: it's the wind. The cats skitter, the dog runs, the hens hide, the ducks alone exult in the storms, and we drink tea and light the fires and wait.

The packing has taken months, and the sheds near the jetty are full of cardboard boxes, bin bags, mail sacks wrapped around garden tools. Three vanloads of belongings have been transported to the north coast already; hundreds of books have travelled in painstaking carrier bags to the mainland, and the cottage is almost empty. More of the family are on hand to help load the boat.

Gus and Sheila joined us for a long and lavish farewell lunch a week earlier, but now Patrick is at his uncle's funeral and I am confined to bed at my mother's house after another operation which converted my partial hysterectomy to a total one. Jon and Claire have left for their winter holiday, and with no human distractions, Gus and Sheila can make their quiet farewells to the island. It is 16 years since they joined Babs, and three decades since they came on a day visit, when the sisters seized on Gus and enticed him to teach Attie wood-turning.

Now it is October, and the wind is rising. The boatman comes an hour early – 'It's now or never!' – they dash about, many belongings stay in the sheds, and there is no time for tears or contemplation. The boat pitches off through the growing sea, and the island is empty for the first time in fifty years.

The houses are dark and cold, and the generator's chatter is silent. The birds possess the island, and the ghosts walk softly down the hill and roam the lawns, the beaches, the old and fallen paths.

Sheila sits in the friendly clutter that she and her family built up on the north coast, before the damp island cottage claimed her, and thinks of the movement of the sea.

Coming back to an empty island, fragile from hospital and crematorium, we totter up the path from the beach and straight into the generator shed. Normally it's run twice a day, but there has been no one to start it for the last 48 hours. Our batteries, as well as Jon's freezer, will be hungry for power.

Patrick turns the key, and nothing happens. The generator is a byword for moodiness, but with both Gus and Jon tending it devotedly over the past few years, it has lulled us into a false sense of security by starting faithfully at every attempt. Now, with a rough crossing and an ebbing tide behind us, we are alone with it and its caprices.

Oh, I think. Really? But Patrick, having tried it a few more times ('Just hold on to that bit there,' he tells me, 'while I try this'), is looking sage.

'I think the control relay connection's shorted,' he muses.

'Ah yes,' I agree, 'the control relay connection. As I suspected.'

'You stay here,' he tells me. 'I'm going to get a torch. And some bits.'

I perch on a diesel can by a wet fuchsia outside the generator shed. I feel too feeble to fret: in the worst case, we have candles, though Jon and Claire could lose a good deal of food. Skipp is worrying, though, as he does when there is a sinister change to his routine; his ears are down and his eyebrows are wrinkled. He looks like Eeyore.

Patrick returns with tools in his hand and a glint in his eye. Skipp and I leave him to it, and collapse morosely on to the sofa, where Patrick joins us, exhausted but smug, with the generator generating. It wasn't, he discovered, a short; the whole control relay has in fact disintegrated. I shake my head: I am not surprised. He has bodged it up with tape, which is the proper island response to such catastrophes. Later, when our usual engineer has sent us the wrong replacement part and Patrick is called upon to develop a more secure solution, he takes the professional approach and bodges it up with string instead.

Patrick adores the need for creative solutions on the island, for applied knowledge, for lateral thinking. The requirement to make do with what we have is liberating: a clean, direct call to action and imagination to maintain basic comforts, food and water, heat and light, without quite the right ingredients or tools. That responsibility is much diminished on the mainland, where expertise and equipment are a call or a click away; here, the urgency of survival, the close relationship with the natural and man-made elements which govern and run one's life, the need for flexibility and adaptation, are exhilarating to us both.

It's true that this is not somewhere you can hide from yourself, but it is possible to be fragile here. When we first came, we were depleted by grief, and desperate for the project of renewal, rebuilding, which the house gave us. But also, every day, there is a moment of joy in the light, the sound of the sea, the blackbird on the lawn; and the howl of the wind is a cleaner demand than the roar of the city.

This is the first place where either of us feels entirely at home.

After Gus and Sheila leave, though, we wonder how well we will manage, quite alone in the winter. With Jon and Claire away on their adventures to France, Turkey, South America, we are in sole charge, until they return once the shortest day is past and the wood is full of violets. We coax the generator into life twice a day, for light and the preservation of the summer's harvest. We count and check the sheep daily, we feed the chickens, we look for storm damage and pump water from the spring. We are content, to our mild surprise and enduring satisfaction, with each other, although we have to relearn the niceties of conversation when we find ourselves with other people again. We are permanently cold and can't access supplies when we want them, or have a bath whenever we might choose to, or order a takeaway, but we have our own rituals and luxuries, and the life we build is anchored, solid, satisfying, until one of us finds they cannot escape a trip away.

So I am here alone.

'Call me if you need me,' says Ernie, more than once, as we unload on to the jetty. We heave ashore bags of groceries, duck food, dog food, parcels from the harbour office, and I take them slowly up to the house on the squeaking sack trolley.

It is winter, but the weather is bizarre.

'It's like a summer's day!' says Ernie on the way over. 'There's a lot of cobwebs about, though,' he adds. 'That means the wind's in the east. But the glass,' he points skywards with a finger, 'it's up.'

Ernie and Patrick are both obsessed with the glass, the barometer; they are both particularly prone to telling me, triumphantly, that the glass is rising; they are both natural optimists and like to be proved right. Today, the implied fine weather is undeniable: I am hot in a T-shirt as I feed the ducks and hens, switch on the generator, make a fuss of the cats.

Generally, we run the generator as it's always been run, in the evening when we want the lights on, but I hate the walk in the dark without a dog, and Skipp has gone to London with Patrick. I run it instead in the afternoon, and scuttle out in the gloaming to switch it off, as late as I dare, with an awkward greeting to Babs beneath her gravestone as I pass.

The evenings are long and quiet and very dark, with only the cats for company. 'Think of Attie,' I say to Ernie in the boat. 'Twelve winters she was here alone, when Babs was ashore teaching.' Down to the generator shed every night in the dark. I know I don't have her courage: if Patrick died (and I regularly poke him in the night to check that he's breathing), I couldn't attempt it alone.

The weather worsens and Patrick is stranded ashore; the foreseeable weather forecast is terrible. The sea is too rough for a boat to come out (this winter, the fishing boats don't go to sea for weeks on end). The only chance he can see to get home is a tide low enough to walk across tomorrow afternoon – in good weather, it would bring adventurers from Looe, but the wind will make the sea level higher, and it's much too cold for a casual wade. I am apprehensive, but Patrick is determined to take his chance. I go to bed alone for what I hope will be the last time for a while, a cat on each side, and dream of tidal waves.

I am on the beach early to look for Patrick: there is distant movement, the figures too far away to make out, but no one else would have come so far down the rocks. When these exceptionally low spring tides occur in clement weather – they traditionally coincide with Good Friday, but can happen at any time of year – there might be three or four days, if the weather is calm enough not to magnify the volume of sea, when you can walk across from Hannafore to the island with no more than wet feet. I have walked it without getting wet at all, and I have attempted it in chest waders and had to turn back when the water reached the top. Patrick will be wearing chest waders now, against the January cold, but Skipp has no such protection.

They have a small send-off committee, including Ernie, who has lent a walking pole. Patrick has brought his own broom handle, so can steady himself on both sides. He steps into the water, and I see Skipp hesitate and then turn back to Ernie, frolicking around him in the manner of a dog wooing a new owner, one with whom he will not have to get extremely cold and wet. I call him, from my sandbank halfway across, and like the obedient dog he is, he follows Patrick into the sea.

Patrick pushes against the water in slow, deliberate steps; Skipp is almost immediately swimming alongside, but, it seems to me, increasingly far away from Patrick. Someone told us it costs £30,000 to train a hearing dog, and I am stricken with guilt by risking not only Skipp, but all that investment, in the winter sea. I hadn't envisaged it like this; I'd imagined they would both walk safely enough, and that the dog would get no more than his legs wet. I have walked out myself to assess the depth, which wasn't much more than knee height on the island side, but they have the worst of it. I call and call the dog, urging him towards me, and he tries and tries. He has become a fair-weather swimmer now that he routinely disembarks the boat over the side and into the water, whatever the season: at some point in September he loses interest in chasing balls into the sea, and doesn't start to paddle again until well into April. In the summer months, he loves splashing about and swimming a few yards to collect a ball, but he tends to panic once he's been in too long. I take him into the water when my brother and his family are staying and have galvanised me into joining them for a swim, and end up raked by his claws when he suddenly realises he's out of his depth and turns to me to get him out.

I wonder how I would save him, if he drifts too far eastwards. Ernie periodically tells us that our chest waders are potentially lethal, and tries to persuade us to invest in wet- or drysuits. I know that the waders I am wearing are at best immobilising in the water, and I also know that many people have died trying to rescue dogs in such circumstances. I can't think about the possibility of needing to rescue Patrick, should he lose his footing on a flat rock slippery with sea lettuce, or a solid one rearing invisibly to knee height to bowl him over. I tell myself he looks powerful, invincible: it is Skipp who looks vulnerable to me, his head only just above water, frighteningly trusting, while Patrick pushes inexorable as the Iron Man through the unfamiliar elements, towards me.

The worst of it, of course, is the middle stretch, equally far from land and land. Skipp has been swimming for minutes already, with the occasional tiny respite on a swell of land or rock, and Patrick is visibly tiring as the water is deeper, more resistant to his legs. They are slowing, and there is really nothing I can do beyond calling to them, urging them both towards me, waiting for the moment when the land will take back Skipp's paws. At last he is staggering through shifting sand and then free into the shallows, rejoicing in the firmer shingle underfoot. We wait for Patrick to catch up, which, inexorable, he soon does, and the three of us walk together through the last stretch of water towards the point of the beach stretching out towards us. I'm not sure which of them to be more worried about: Skipp is very wet, and must be very cold, but is dashing round the beach with his back end shooting right underneath him; Patrick is largely clad in rubber, but will be badly fatigued by working against the water. Rubbed down and tucked in front of the gas fire, Skipp soon revives, and Patrick takes to the sofa and feels the odd weightlessness of his limbs, supported and in the air.

Home, relearning the space, Skipp reaches the bottom of the path, and pauses. Something has changed on the beach: the certainty has gone out of it. There is a drop, half the height of a Labrador, from the concrete end of the path which used to drift into sand. Below, his paws touch rock, not sand, and the smells at the top of the beach are no longer trees and old seaweed but bare rock, great boulders twice his size and many times his weight thrown against the crumbling cliff by the sea.

The beach is huge. At its point, where waves meet waves, spray explodes at each break, fountaining exuberantly into the air. He dashes forward, glances behind him, and when the release command comes – 'Off you go!' – he whirls round, pounces on a piece of seaweed, and is off to experience this extraordinary new land, bounding over the white shingle to the point where the two seaward sides of the beach meet, twice as far away now as it ever has been, the beach reconfigured from oblong to triangle. He stops well short of the implacable waves, battling it out between north and east.

Walking on round the island, there are gobbets of foam everywhere: 150 feet up at the top of the hill, among the trees in the wood. On the path to the south of the house, not far from a cliff edge, the grass is so covered with spray and foam that it looks like snow. Skipp disapproves of this; he doesn't like things that feel odd under his paws (tarpaulins, manhole covers, the metal steps to an aircraft), and works his way carefully around it.

Inside the house, the wind groans and complains like a noisy hypochondriac. In the corner of our sitting room where I work, with windows in front and at my side, it is at its loudest, and I feel oppressed by it after a couple of days with no let-up. I am working full-time for the business now, at the dining table for 10-, 11-, 12-hour days. As the client base expands and employee numbers creep upwards, I slot myself into various gaps that need to be filled.

There was never enough time when I didn't have a job for all that needed to be done to keep the damp at bay in the house, and the gardens productive, and now I start to feel a kind of panic wherever I look. As the house silts up with clutter and dog hair, and the vegetable patches with nettles, bindweed, grasses, I feel the constant reproach, the imagined spectator muttering, 'How can they live like this?' I think of Babs and Attie, shutting all comers out of the house as the chaos slowly rose.

We are the first people, I think, to live here full-time with full-time jobs which aren't integral to island life, and it is an odd mix. I start to long for some of the luxuries of modern life we'd happily turned our backs on: being able to pay someone else to make you a cup of coffee, on your way to work, or not having to cook because there are takeaways, pubs, ready meals. More potently, I miss the early days of being here, the quiet pace of island-focused life: steadily bringing in wood, cutting back brambles, repainting damp walls, making bread. At the weekends, we sleep and work, and time becomes, again, a precious commodity; more precious in an environment which is not geared to that sad contemporary group, the time-poor.

We still spend more time outdoors than we used to, with tea breaks in the sunshine, and the commute is trouble-free. In the winter, in the gales, there is a comfort in the supremacy of wind, the impossibility of taming it. Storms last for spectacular days: Patrick and I stand in the doorway one afternoon, open-mouthed, as first Little Island and then the flagpole between us and it disappear under waves and spray at the high tide.

*

Ernie turns 80, and every time he goes to the doctor, we panic. He looks like a fit 60-year-old, and is stronger than either of us, but he is starting to drop hints about independence, and so we buy a boat.

This will be our fourth boat. The first three are inflatables: first Graham's little boat, and then Vernon's *Moonstone*, which survives everything we throw at her and is still waiting, deflated, in the big shed. For a season or two, we nip back and forwards with her quite successfully; I have a temporary job collecting unreturned 2011 censuses, and Patrick picks me up regularly from the rocks at Hannafore, where Ross went into the sea for his night-time swim.

We are now cautious about the sea state, but still learning about navigation. Once you've got safely off the beach, then unless the tide is very low, the stretch of open water between us and the harbour mouth is straightforward enough, and you'd have to try quite hard to run into another boat, but as you turn alongside the pier towards the harbour, there are more hazards. Travelling alone in our first, tiny inflatable boat, to meet me ashore for a rare night out, Patrick's attention, once he's successfully crossed the first stretch of water, is on the harbour 'bar', where sea meets river; often the most difficult part of the journey to or from the island, especially in a south-east wind and at an ebb tide. Much larger vessels can rear out of the water at almost 90 degrees as they push through it, slapping down on to the water before being pushed straight back up. He gives scant attention to Nailzee Rock, where there is a metal mast to warn boats returning to harbour, but the little rubber boat is hopelessly attracted to it.

Patrick hears and feels the calamity as the outboard's shearing pin snaps on one of the steel guide wires attached to the mast. His instinct is to improvise a fix, but the little boat is tossing alarmingly on the swell of water over the bar: sitting still is not a wise option, and he settles down to row.

Perhaps it is 600 yards over the bar and up the river to a safe mooring point, but it is against the current, and Patrick's muscles, even in a period of relative fitness, are not made for rowing. His character, though, is not made for despair. 'How hard can it be?' he asks himself, embarking on the row, finding that if he slackens he is pushed back out to sea – and an hour later his muscles tell him just how hard. Uncompromising determination sees him safely into harbour, but we opt to stay in Looe that night.

We envy Jon and Claire's independence, with their kayaks, and the fuss-free system they have established of tucking them into the van they keep parked on Hannafore. We couldn't carry kayaks around the headland to the cottage, so Patrick decides that an inflatable version is the answer; we could easily manage a two-man inflatable kayak between us. His sporty friend Mark joins him, for the maiden voyage, and Patrick shows me proud photos of the kayak in action.

We take it out for the first time together after an island party with the friends we used to convene with in London for

Christmas dinner, who congregate a couple of times on the island for 'Summermas'. After the turkey burgers and shaved sprout salad, they set off with Ernie for Looe's Festival of the Sea, and we follow them in the kayak. We begin smartly, in time with each other, making good headway through the water, and about thirty feet off the island, we capsize. Ridiculously, we are wearing the chest waders which Ernie warned us against, and which immediately immobilise us. Paddles, clothes and the waterproof box with valuables all float off in different directions, and both they and we have to wait for an ignominious rescue by a group of proper kayakers, who tow us to shore and round up our belongings.

As Ernie ages, Patrick's fitness declines. A new drug gives him a good year, but is discontinued for use. It is a drug originally used for glaucoma, which now has better, newer options for treatment, and it is not worth the manufacturers' while to keep producing it for a small cohort of patients with 'periodic paralysis', of which group Patrick's Andersen–Tawil syndrome is one disorder, though we fight for years to get hold of it. His hospital stay the year of my hysterectomy, our third year on the island, becomes an annual event, and his stamina decreases as various manifestations of partial paralysis increase in frequency.

A kayak, then, is no longer a possibility for him, and we also now need a boat with a solid floor, to accommodate Skipp's claws. We find one on eBay, a 14-foot fibreglass boat with an outboard, a smaller version of *Pania* or a larger, more solid take on *Moonstone*. We're delighted to discover that it's at the boatyard in Looe, and take it out for a test drive. Skipp is reluctant to get in, but we lure him with biscuits, and swoop successfully around the bay. We discuss winches and running moorings: 'I'll sort you out a winch,' the seller assures us, 'I'll make up a trolley.' We know that the challenge will be in manoeuvring up and down the beach – inflatable *Moonstone* is heavy enough; the two of us can only just manage her.

At the point where we pay, we have a winch but only half the amount of cable we need to pull the boat in. We host a summer party for our colleagues, and while some of us sit on the sand with a wind-up gramophone, drinking beer, Patrick and his business partner Justin take the boat out for its first outing. We have no idea it will also be its last. We are excited about this new chapter in our seagoing lives; we have called the boat *Quarll*, after a Robinson Crusoe-like fictional figure who has given his name to my mother's most recent book of poems, as she has given us the money to buy the boat.

It takes four of us to haul it back up the beach, and we don't have the conjunction of time and manpower to try again that summer. The seller evades calls, messages and visits, the cable and trolley do not materialise, and the winter storms bury the winch completely under sand and boulders.

When we first came to the island, Gus and Sheila had recently been given a little boat: a pretty, white open boat along the lines of the clinker-built ferries of Looe. It sat tied to the railings at the top of the beach, anchored to the bottom of the path, and we never saw it on the water: in time, it was taken further up and filled with flowers outside the tractor shed. We couldn't understand it: it was the perfect boat. Why on earth did Gus never take it out, enjoy being independent of boatmen? Island-dwellers had always, of course, had boats: why didn't he use his?

Perhaps he was ashamed, as we are, of lacking the physical strength to manoeuvre her. Island-dwellers need either physical strength, or the money to pay for someone else's. Gus was in his late seventies when we arrived, and weakened by a recent, vicious bout of shingles, and Patrick and I, by the time of *Quarll*, are depleted physically too. We are reliant on *Quarll*'s seller to make launching and hauling up possible; we are reliant on goodwill and professional pride, and infuriated by that reliance. We should have tried again, of course, in the spring; dug out the winch from its sandy grave; found another engineer; got the boat into the water. We would have, once, we would have fought; but the fight is going out of us.

Quarll sits under a tarpaulin in the wood for two years before we sell her on.

Summer buffers up against autumn with a jolt, this particular year, six weeks of blue skies abruptly clouding, the advent of wind and rain coinciding with the last of our guests. Patrick's sister's children, edging into their teens, return quickly from blackberrying, shrimping and dog-walking forays, to dry their clothes in front of the woodburner and play endless games of Island-opoly and gin rummy. Each visits us separately over the summers, self-sufficient with two or three friends, but there is something very comfortable about the three of them together.

Once they've left, the disobliging weather swings round again to innocent blue skies and warmth, for the last, lovely day of August. It is not enough to cheer Patrick, who is in pain, and while I chatter about butchers and apple-pressing, and move the pigs into the top of the orchard to forage for windfalls in their last week, he is silent; he doesn't even smile when the pigs escape on to the lawn, scattering the ducks in their pen and alarming the custard-coloured dog.

Three weeks ago, getting out of bed, Patrick said, 'I've got funny foot.' 'Funny foot' appears once or twice a month; 'funny face' slightly less often; being 'broken' in one way or another happens now almost daily. This funny foot seems worse than usual: it is a sort of cramp or spasm, which leaves him hobbling around for a few hours, but this time it's agony to put any weight on it, and the following morning the pain is so bad that he cancels a work call and spends the day in bed; this is almost unheard of.

He consults his doctor sister, who suggests external heat and internal tonic water, for quinine to combat cramps; he consults the specialist nurse in London, and on her advice the local GP; we are sent to Casualty in Plymouth, where we spend four hours jumping through the hoops of X-rays and blood tests before they give up on us. The GP prescribes painkillers and anti-inflammatories, and suggests tendonitis, but the next day it is suddenly better.

Patrick spends three days, this year (last year, a week – next year, who knows?), in the neurological hospital in London. I wait on the island with the sad dog, and receive sad bulletins from Patrick.

'They think it may be something else,' he says. He's played them a video of his twitching hand. 'There's only been one other person with my condition who's had that.'

He has to go back for more MRI scans, more ECGs.

'I feel like I'm in limbo,' he says.

We try to cut down on trips ashore to see clients, family, doctors, but there are obligations it is hard to ignore. The sea state is unpredictable, especially in the winter – you can look out on what seems to be a flattish expanse of water, but once you are on it, or negotiating embarkation from the beach or crossing the harbour bar, you realise how quietly violent it is. We consider the conditions for a winter dentist's appointment – Patrick's wisdom teeth are causing problems – and decide it's manageable. Ernie is the ultimate arbiter: if he says a crossing isn't possible, we don't argue, but he is also obliging, and will try to get us ashore when we ask him to.

Today, it is borderline. Before now, in rough seas, Ernie has warned us, 'She'll go broadside, and then we've had it!' but his judgement and skill have combined so that this has never been on the cards. Now, with all of us aboard, his boat has swung round at right angles to sit alongside the beach, and pushing her off with the two paddles is not enough. I jump back into the sea to haul her round, waiting for an incoming wave to give us a chance of floating before we all heave to, but we're making no impact.

'We're going to have to phone Jon,' I say. 'Or the lifeboat,' says Ernie, but none of us can reach our phones. After the third or fourth try, Patrick realises why we're not moving. 'You're pushing the wrong way!' he roars at me. 'I'm pushing the way I always push!' I tell him, but we're usually pushing to stop her swinging round in the first place, to keep the prow pointing into the beach. It's quite obvious to the two on the boat that now we've come halfway round, the requirement is to swing to the left again, to point towards the mainland, but this kind of spatial reasoning is not my strong point.

When we stop working against each other, she shifts after a couple more tries, and Ernie can use the engine to move the boat safely back into the water. I stand for a minute: are they coming back for me, or should Patrick go on alone? They gesture unintelligibly; I decide that, either way, I need to get out of the waders. Ernie was already there when I arrived at the beach, and I didn't wait to get the straps over my shoulders; the waders have now slipped down to my waist, and are overflowing with water, which means that I can't move.

If you stand sideways to a wave, you're less of a target, more likely to stay upright as it breaks around you. A little swell adds excitement to a summer swim; you wade out through breakers to catch a big one and body-surf it back to the beach. Now, unable to move my feet, the sensation is not quite excitement; there is no real drama, I think, I'm too close to the shore to drown. I stay where I am, sideways to the waves, and kick my way out of my waders in the water; I drag myself and them to land and drop the waders above the high-tide mark. Turning to look back out to sea, I am sure that I will see *Pania* heading for the mainland; but she is coming back for me.

Ernie holds her a little way off the beach, and I wade out to chest height and try to get my foot in the bottom rung of the ladder. I think I will be safe then, but with the curve to the boat's side, I'm leaning back too far to get a purchase to push my other foot up effectively. Patrick leans over the side, holding my hands, but I just don't have the strength to get any further up the ladder.

'Pull her up, Patrick!' yells Ernie, and to me, 'Get your other foot on the ladder!'

Patrick and I are frozen in what looks like a life-or-death embrace, except that there is only four foot of water under me. Eventually, Ernie loses patience, abandons the tiller and heaves me in himself: I flop on to the bench seat along the side of the boat like an exhausted cod, and lie there, panting, completely unable to move.

After a couple of minutes, I summon the energy to sit up, and take Patrick's hand. 'Should we get you to a doctor?' I ask him.

Funny foot is a regular occurrence now, and the pain in the muscles of his thighs, his arms, his shoulders is worse. It occurs to me that this exertion might actually kill him. He refuses a doctor, of course, until a week later, when the pain is unbearable and even he can see he needs help.

For now, we sit wetly in the boat, with Skipp shivering uncontrollably next to us, and concentrate on not being sick, while Ernie issues an edict, a non-negotiable, permanent ban, on ever wearing chest waders for getting on a boat again.

We thought we might be lonely. We thought we would miss things, people: our friends, our families, baths, pubs, newspapers. We wondered how our relationship would survive the intense togetherness, and how manageable a new business would be without a mainstream internet connection or reliable access to clients. We worried, for the first few years, whether the business was sustainable, whether we could make enough money to live on, whether we might have to call it a day and go and get proper jobs again; then, we were too busy to worry. We weren't sure we could get the house habitable within a season, whether Patrick's plans for wiring and plumbing and solar power would really work. We knew we were dependent on the goodwill of others, and the good behaviour of boats. We blessed Ernie daily.

We weren't concerned about the sheer physical effort involved in bringing everything we needed across ourselves: on to the boat, off the boat, up the path to the house. We were blasé about the aspects of life which our great-grandparents might have warned us about, the daily grind of bringing wood in, managing our small crops and livestock, spring-cleaning when everything is covered in soot. Patrick had just turned forty when we came to Island House, I wasn't there yet; we knew we'd had more energy twenty years before but essentially, we still felt invincible.

But we now know that soon, in a few months or years, we will have to leave; before living here becomes a penance instead of a challenge. We will leave the beaches and rocks, the hill and the wood; we will leave the house in good heart, restored, to become a place for holidays or the home of someone we don't know, who'll exult in the view from the bathroom, the flagstone floors, the light pouring in through the bay window. We will leave the familiar ghosts to be a flicker in the peripheral vision of people who don't recognise them, and the damp for someone else to address. We will come here less often by boat, but more in dreams, walking the flower-lined path towards the white gable end, half hidden in the fuchsia hedge. We will begin a new life, a softer life, perhaps, in another house, and we will never quite get over the fact of not being here.

Chapter 16
Christmas

---

the only time here on the island
in midwinter, since they live
so scattered over the globe.

Chris Considine, *Christmas dinner*

'Have you been leaving mangoes lying around?'

My brother Paul has phoned, and this is his opening gambit. Mangoes, I think. Mangoes . . .

'Mangoes?'

I am playing for time. Paul's children are particularly fond of mangoes; could he be referring to a mango I bought for them and then – forgot? Left behind a radiator? Is his flat enduring mango poisoning of some sort?

'Mangoes,' he confirms. 'Or any other ripe fruit?'

'Ah.' It makes sense. 'You mean the OFB.'

Paul's irreverent nickname for my mother is the Old Fruit

Bat, and when she does something particularly batty, he blames it on too much ripe fruit.

'She really has lost it this time.' We agree on this.

She has emailed both of us, requesting a response URGENTLY, suggesting that she should hire a helicopter in order to transport everyone to the island at Christmas. It's Paul's fault – John and his family have simply said that they'll get here, even if they have to wade chest-deep, but Paul has suggested that his six-month-old baby will only be allowed to make the boat trip in the most clement of weather, and the weather in December is rarely clement. Patrick and I are inured to the vicissitudes of the weather; experience has taught us that it's simply a waste of energy to worry about it three or four weeks hence, for no forecast can give one any real clue at that distance.

But my mother is a worrier, and likes her environment calm and controlled. If we are all planning to spend Christmas on the island, then she wants to make sure that we really will all be there. She has had an estimate from a local helicopter firm, and has offered to pay.

'But if the weather's too bad,' points out Patrick, 'a helicopter wouldn't be able to land either.' In the end, we agree that she will buy the baby a life jacket instead, and we will put our faith in Ernie and, if backup is called for, his grandson Jamie, and the helicopter is stood down.

I am still surprised that we have got this far. 'Wouldn't it be nice,' I suggested, steely-toned, to both my brothers during their summer visits, 'for us all to have Christmas here this year?' Paul is in Edinburgh now, but may not be in a year's time; John has once or twice brought his family from Canada for an English Christmas and might, I think, be persuaded to again, with the lure of the island in winter, but not more than once in the next few years. This is our best chance: I put my case forcefully and, unexpectedly, they both accede.

Family Christmases dissolved after my parents' divorce, when I was eight, and John left home in my early teens, taking with him any hopes of Christmas together with even one parent. When my mother bought her house in Yorkshire, she summoned her children to join her for her first Christmas there, but that was 23 years ago.

At 13, riding a recalcitrant pony through the flat Bedfordshire landscape; in my twenties, having root canal treatment; in my thirties, fretting about my father's health, my favourite soothing fantasy detailed the Christmas I would one day have with my own family: rituals of decoration, carol-singing, merrymaking with my imaginary children.

The front doors have wreaths of holly and bay, and all the fires are lit. Smugglers Cottage, transformed like a stage set from dereliction to comfort, is crowded with candles; and in the bunk room in Jetty Cottage there are fairy lights glinting in bed frames, curtain rails, a washing line. The cured hind leg of one of the summer's pigs lies heavily in the freezer, the

Christmas Eve ham. There are paper chains and mince pies, a tree leaning up against the gate outside, home-made crackers and several bottles of port. In the spare bedroom is a tiny glass filled with early violets, and a rocking chair to which my mother can retreat.

The weather is kind enough. The Canadians arrive without incident; the following day, conditions for the Austro-Scots, as John has christened them, are rougher, but nothing for which dry socks and Metaxa brandy can't compensate. Calamity is only narrowly averted, though, as the turkey, of all things, is left on the boat, and Ernie has to come back in to the beach in seas which on most days would in truth have been too rough to come out in.

They are all ensconced for Christmas Eve, to decorate the tree together, eat the ham, toast many toasts with the Prosecco John has provided. The children, under teenage Nicholas's supervision, clean out the chickens and hunt for duck eggs. They run and run, on grass and sand, and John swims in the December sea. At midnight on Christmas Eve, he and Sylvia borrow a bible and walk up the hill to the chapel site to make their observances. A row of stockings, sewn by Patrick from oddments of fabric with initials in felt, hangs above the Esse in the kitchen, and in the cottages, those who are awake hear a faint jingle and a heavy footstep as the stockings are delivered to those for whom they are intended. Paul and I meet in the dark early morning of Christmas Day, to stoke the Esse and put the turkey in, and then go back to our chocolate oranges and the first storm of wrapping paper as the stuffed stockings go limp again.

The dog is terribly sick in the early afternoon of Christmas Day, from licking up turkey and bacon fat which has spilled from an inadequate tray, slid through the inadequate seal on the oven door and pooled temptingly on the kitchen flagstones. This is unnoticed until we start to mobilise for Christmas dinner, at which point Nicholas steps in something wet. Extensive cleaning delays the food even longer: my mother is ravenous, the children overexcited, the dog in disgrace; I am exhausted and cross. John spends endless hours washing up, and my mother spends longer than she had sociably planned sitting quiet in her rocking chair. The noise from the children is incessant, the house is too small, the beer runs out, everyone's patience frays.

But on Christmas afternoon, the vomit removed, the adventuring turkey carved, I can feel nothing but love, looking down the table to the bay window and the windswept garden beyond. Baby Malise, having recently discovered solid food, steals sausages and carrots from his mother's plate; John slips the coin he finds in his Christmas pudding to eight-year-old Finbarr on his left. Later, we introduce Nicholas and Sylvia to Trivial Pursuit, and are beaten hollow by the Canadians. Gus goes quite quietly to bed, for a five-year-old so full of marshmallows and chocolate, and lies awake with his mother for a little, gazing at the fairy lights: 'Magical,' Jay says.

They all leave together, the day after Boxing Day, from the jetty. We fill the boat with children and bags, quickly, unsentimental against the swell of the sea. Patrick and I watch the familiar boat and wave, until the little, low figures are indistinguishable, and then we take each other's hands and walk up the steps with the yellow dog between us, back up to the house.

Chapter 17
Ashore

The pig's long back, scored and furrowed –
its rounded hillocks and slopes like the Cornish landscape –
is browning and shining between two rows
of little flames

Chris Considine, *Hog-roast*

My mother, still struggling to adapt to living in a city after twenty years in her remote house in the Dales, is worried when the flats above and below her go on sale. She hasn't lived in a flat for decades, and last time she did, she lay awake for furious hours on many hot nights, in thrall to noisy neighbours. She is mourning her wild hillside, struggling with the convenience of city life: doctors, dentists and shops within walking distance, so there is no need to drive, and the problems with her eyes, her sight, become an inconvenience rather than a disaster. Having decided to leave the house and the miles of moor she loved, she chose to come to the city nearest to her only UK-based child, and we looked at several sensible semis before she bought the flat, with its high Victorian ceilings and magnificent outlook on to Plymouth Sound, on a whim. Now, reminded why a semi would have been sensible, she is terrified that the new owners of the basement flat below hers, and the studio above her bedroom, will disturb her. Having downsized considerably, she has money in the bank, and she buys them both.

As she needs to fit in whole families of relations from Australia and Canada, she keeps hold of the basement and lets out the tiny first-floor flat to a charming, and quiet, Italian girl. With the basement spruced up to her requirements, she is keen for it to be used, and after five winters on the island, we decide to spend a few weeks, in the January after our family island Christmas, road-testing it, and enjoying the comforts of heating, hot water, baths and pubs.

For the first week, Patrick feels marvellous. The heat is wonderfully soothing to his muscles, and for several days he is almost pain-free. We know it's often the case that a change like this helps for a week or so and then loses its magic, and so we're philosophical when the pain starts to return. We're disconcerted when it gets worse: by the time we've been back on the island a couple of weeks, it's unbearable. We spend more weeks fighting 'computer says no' receptionists; we come ashore; the GP gives Patrick liquid morphine, which helps for a day or two; and finally she manages to get through to the neurological consultant who Patrick is 'under' in London, and he is admitted to the specialist London hospital. By this time, he can barely get out of bed.

Skipp and I visit him every day in hospital, the dog packed in among pushchairs and angry feet for an hour's bus ride each way from the friends and relations we stay with. When we first go in, Patrick is lying on his bed with computer and phone beside him, untouched: I have never seen him too ill for technology.

We spend a dispiriting, infuriating three weeks like this. On the first day, the registrar tells me it's probably psychological. We hold out great hope for a visit from the Big Cheese himself: is this really Andersen syndrome, which we'd understood wasn't typified by this kind of pain; what else could it be; if other Andersen's patients *have* had this kind of pain, what happened next? His answer is literally a shrug: 'Well – we know you've got Andersen's – we've not found anything else . . .' Shrug.

Patrick is discharged to his local pain team, and started on some morphine-type patches, plus tramadol, codeine, paracetamol, naproxen (another painkiller), gabapentin (another painkiller), omeprazole (to stop him feeling sick from all the painkillers) and sertraline (for depression).

We go home for the summer. Patrick can no longer walk to the beach; he can no longer walk the thirty feet to the shed, without pain. Cognitively, he's dulled from a combination of drugs and pain. The business struggles, as Justin and I try to cover for some of what Patrick can't do.

*

I phone my brother in Edinburgh: 'Can't you come and fix that knackered tractor?' A friend has revamped the engine of the little tractor which has been quietly rusting away under an old pig ark: if we could coax the bodywork into life, at least Patrick could leave the house. Paul has a better idea.

'We'll buy him a quad bike.'

'Absolutely, definitely not,' I tell him, so he arrives six weeks later with a small, shiny red quad bike, which Ernie's son Philip and his mate Angus make light work of lifting off the boat. Patrick loves it: he is once more a crucial part of loading and unloading stuff from boats, roaring up on the quad bike to the beach or the jetty to transport heavy shopping or bags of animal feed.

Ashore for an eight-week pain-management course in Plymouth in the autumn, we then go home for what we know has to be our last winter stint, alone with the weather and the sheep for a couple of months before Christmas. By the time we get back from sitting out the rest of the winter ashore, the quad bike has seized up and Patrick's freedom is over.

We know we will have to leave. We have an offer accepted on a barn for conversion down an almost impassable track at the edge of Bodmin Moor, above our favourite village of Minions, but realise eventually that the vendor has no intention of selling. We have another offer accepted on a more complicated wreck of a house further north, near Camelford, but a rival bidder eventually beats us. After a year of negotiating with estate agents and poring over property pages, I catch sight of an unprepossessing pink house in an area of north Devon we don't know. It has eight acres and failed to sell at auction, and we drive straight back to the estate agent's after our viewing and make an offer.

By the spring, just over a year since Patrick's life changed, we have builders lined up to renovate the new house – another project. We also have Patrick's father as project manager, and we don't realise just how essential this will be when we take up his offer. It must be finished by September, we tell everyone. That's the latest we can leave the island, the latest the weather is anything like reliable enough to plan furniture removal, or forgiving enough for Patrick to cope with the vicissitudes of island life.

Ashore, Patrick has given in to a wheelchair. On the island, we are reliant on Jon's help with unloading gas bottles or anything else too heavy for me and Ernie to unload alone, and also for ferrying Patrick to and from the boat, when necessary, in his tractor.

Winter caretaking needs planning, now, and arrangements need to be made for someone else to be on the island when Jon and Claire are ashore. Patrick and I have agreed to cover a few days in February, but Patrick isn't well enough to come with me, so as the previous island-sitter takes my place in the boat, I am alone on the island, on the day of the family funeral which Sheila and their children hold for Gus ten days after his death.

When they left the island, Gus relaxed happily into his old home on the north Cornwall coast, overlooking Lundy, watching the garden birds from his kitchen window with complete delight. He wound down very slowly over a couple of years, sleeping more and more, becoming infirm, remaining content.

The eccentric basset hound Edward waited until he had gone, and a fortnight later he gave up too, rudderless without his immutable distrust of Gus.

Starting up the generator for its evening roar, I sense Gus behind me in the shed, a benign presence making sure I'm handling the switches safely. As I walk up the path, I think I can hear him humming his way along it ahead of me, just out of sight. But when I tie the flag to the flagpole in the stiff February breeze, looking back over the springy turf towards the rising slope of the island, and settle it at half-mast, the island is empty, nothing but sky and sea, and the gulls wheeling against the sun.

We come back in April, for a final summer at home. In July, it's our tenth wedding anniversary, six and a half years after we came to the island, and despite previous weather-related failures, we decide that the double excuse for a party is too compelling to pass up. We invite family, local friends, friends from upcountry; we make bunting, hire glasses, negotiate the logistics of boat trips; and incredibly, the weather remains fair.

Our pig guru, Chris, has recently branched out into hog roasts, and we know he will be game to bring the whole kit and caboodle out to the island. He opts to come out with a friend in a small boat, slightly misjudges the time, and tears across the bay to the beach with the metal roaster precariously perched on the back of the boat. As Jon and I wade in to take possession of it, I find myself eye to eye with the pig coffined inside, and think, thank goodness it's this way round: vegetarian Jon might have found that sudden eyeballing a step too far.

'I was going to stay and get it going for you for an hour,' Chris says, as we puff up the slope to the space across the path from Smugglers Cottage where we've agreed with Jon that the pig can slow-cook overnight, 'but we're going to run out of water to get back in to Looe. So I'll light it for you, then you need to watch it for an hour with the burners on low, then turn it right down.' Ten minutes later he's gone, and I, having thought the pig would look after itself, and flat out with the inevitable last-minute rush of party preparations, wonder how the hell I can give an hour to this.

My mother is 75 now, but could be taken for ten years younger. 'Could you watch the pig for an hour?' I ask her, and condemn her to a solitary vigil in a stiff breeze, willing the burners to stay low but on. I tell her often that such adventures keep her young.

She has been an invaluable support to us. Could you come the day before the party, Mother, and help us clean? Could you roast a hog? Lend us a thousand pounds for a few weeks? Island- and animal-sit for several days? Could we come and stay for seven months? She is undemonstrative but present, clear on her parameters, and her help comes with no implied requirement for gratitude, for appreciation of the trouble she is going to: it is the absolute best sort of help, and we know we are lucky.

Guests begin to arrive around midday. My school friend Katie is straight into the kitchen to assemble magnificent pavlovas and trifles. Patrick's nephews, Sam and Ben, take on waiter duties with aplomb, setting fish boxes full of bottles of home-made elderflower champagne, a drink for which the sisters were famous, in the sea to cool; splashing hurriedly out to retrieve them when they start to float away. Ernie comes ashore, which is rare, with his wife Margaret, lifeboatman grandson Jamie, daughter Katrina, and they hobnob on the beach with Sheila, back for the first time since she left the island, and with our best Looe allies – Margaret from the chemist, Chris from the Spar, Carolyn who supplies straw for our pigs. Again, the island pulls together all the stages of my life, and of Patrick's: family, school and university friends – Martin, of course – friends from our London lives, from my teaching career – both colleagues and students, for two incorrigible sixth-formers I taught over a decade ago have stayed in touch. Skipp's trainer comes to the party; our Looe friends; friends of my mother's from Plymouth. Our carefully curated playlist – from 'My Funny Valentine' to 'Perfect Day' – is mellowed by the calls of gulls, floating blissful on their currents of warm air. Sam moves from waiter duties to card tricks and the hog is demolished. When we talk to people now about that day, the first thing they remember is the hog, never mind the location or the company – 'That crackling . . .'

Children are in and out of the sea as the boats begin to take our guests back to the mainland, and I almost glimpse myself with them, shy and fascinated as a half-tamed pony as the unassuming boats become suddenly stern and solid from a swimmer's perspective, rearing high-sided out of the water to eyes at keel height. The beach empties, but some of the exodus is to the house, to the lit and decorated lawn; tents spill into the sheep pen below, and we count 40 guests overnight.

The manpower is too good an opportunity to miss – we have a project which we have calculated will need eight strong men. In the garden are two huge, carved hexagonal stones: Attie's book relates that she found them on the beach, and getting them transported up to the house would have been some achievement. Also in the garden is a granite structure which she described firmly as the 'font' from the chapel, but which Sheila recognises when she sees a picture in a book catalogue showing a large stone ornament from a Japanese garden. When we realise that adding the two hexagonal stones, the larger on top, will make our edifice look exactly like the one in the catalogue, we are keen to put it all together. My brothers and John's teenage son Nicholas came very close, once, to doing so, using wood as levers in the best tradition of pyramid-building or Esse-moving, but were ultimately beaten: the weight is colossal and the sturdiest wood snaps. Eight is the largest number of people you could get round the stone, and the eight strongest men self-select, after our beach party, and succeed, miraculously, in assembling the structure.

It is late by the time supper is eaten and most of the washing-up done, but I sit then on the dark lawn with my friends, and I think it is Gerard – stalwart of Summermas, and father of my godson Robin – who first sees the shooting stars, glorious in the sky, flaming through the forty years of my love for this place, and these people.

We start to pack. We spend a day of my brother John's annual stay with his family emptying the shed, bringing boxful after boxful as offerings to Patrick on the lawn, to make judgements about all those things that might have come in handy and might still here, or at our new house, or – hardest decision – are no longer useful, and for the chop. My mother comes for one of her quietly heroic visits, and helps me to pack books and sheets and crockery over a long weekend. Patrick's parents come for the day, to empty the understairs cupboard and reorganise the shed, enormously energetic as always. We are in a welter of lists and boxes, and every weekend is spent packing, and every hour after work when I can lift my head.

We still have 21 ducks to move. We planned to leave our five ducks behind, to live out a dignified retirement, and Jon and Claire have agreed to feed and keep an eye on them, but we have had a population explosion over the summer. We thought we were safe, with both the deliberate and the accidental drakes in the flock now gone, but the wild mallards have other ideas. Spare mallard drakes have always appeared in the spring, but haven't stayed long, but the drake who turns up this year is looking for long-term wifelets and an easy billet. He is brazen, greedy, misogynist. With a Bill and Hillary already in the flock, we name him Donald. We spend weeks waving brooms at him – the ducks think this makes you a monstrous bird with a terrifying wing span – and chasing him out of their pen, but it's my nephew Nicholas, 16 now, who finally sees him off via a patient campaign with a water pistol. We search for nests, and find all but one; all but one of the ducks come home, and we relax, until the day I hear squeaking coming from the pond, and find the missing black duck Nigella teaching her 16 children how to swim.

Miraculously, all of them survive, and, equally miraculously, we manage to find a smallholding prepared to take the lot, unsexed at about eight weeks old. We start to feed them in our largest pig crate, with a string tied to the handle, but it takes three goes to get them all rounded up. The youngsters and the younger ducks go off together; the oldest three – our favourite original, seven-year-old Bill, and the two pure-bred Indian Runners, which Gus so liked, Puddleduck and Lil – go to live with Sheila and her daughter Jane, where they settle immediately on the spacious pond, in the windswept fields.

*

I start to dream, as the initial alarm of Patrick's illness shades into routine, about lying on the grass near the duck pen and sinking gently into the ground. I picture this often, a quiet absorption into the earth with the sounds of birds around me, and it has a familiar kind of comfort, the comfort of trees and the earth.

After a year, with our departure planned, the picture changes. I imagine walking out into the sea: sliding in from the jetty, pushing slowly through the green water. I can imagine just how the water will look as I drop gently into it, how it will cut and sway around me. I know how it will sound, the suck and splash, the interrupted rhythm as I disturb it, the swishing sound as I walk, then swim, the soft sounds of solitude and vastness which surrounded Ross as he set off into the sea, looking for something he couldn't name.

A recurring, gallows-humour half-joke for me and Patrick, when things seem particularly dark, is for one of us to say to the other: 'Is it time to top ourselves?' The ritual answer is 'Skippy wouldn't like it.' I know that the idea has crossed Patrick's mind, when the pain has been unbearable, but I know also that he is too brave, too kind, too responsible. For myself, worn out in those sad, exhausted final weeks on the island, I feel not a violent rush of active despair, but the appeal of sliding slowly out of sight, into the earth or the water.

When I can't sleep, walking myself mentally round the island is too sad, now, and I think instead of how I will plant the garden at our new house: roses and peonies, delphiniums and stocks. One night shortly before we are due to leave, future flowers are not enough, and I look to the physicality of the island for help. I get out of bed and go outside and across the lawn, through the garden gate on to the wild grey grass running down the hill, through the sheep pen, round to the jetty and down the steps.

It is a misty night, and the mainland ahead of me is the dimmest of horizons, its familiar lights invisible. Jetty Beach stretches away to my left, topped by the run of silent, black trees, and the world is monochrome. The beach has always been one of my favourite places on the island, a benign and sheltered spot without the bleakness and grandeur of the west side, of High Cove and the outer reaches of Gull Island. Its rocks are low and rounded and the sand is yellow: it is a place for hobbits, not for warriors, and just sitting on the jetty next to it is comforting. It is a high-ish tide, and my boots meet the water; when I relax and let my legs dangle, they fill with it, and feel at home.

There are little moving lights glinting on the sea in front of me. They remind me of shooting stars. Perhaps, I think, it could be phosphorescence? I've never seen it, this weird phenomenon, elusive as the Northern Lights, though my mother remembers swimming in it in the island's sea at night, forty years ago. Is it a sign? And if so, of what?

It is not a sign, I realise, and feel a little foolish. It is Jon walking down the path to turn off the generator. I sit for a while, swinging my legs gently, and watch the reflected lights come back along the path as Jon goes in to bed.

Once the light has gone and the sky breathes peacefully around me again, the water is greyer, quieter than I'd pictured, less fractured. I ease myself gently to the seabed, and stand in the water up to my thighs: it is lovely, cool and quiet. I stand for a minute, or more, and then start to walk very slowly away from the land. I am not going anywhere in particular, but it is so calm in the sea; I would like to stay here, to melt into it. I luxuriate in its coldness, its softness, the small noises of its dreams in the darkness.

The meeting of sea and land, the liminal shore, defines the island. It is the place of uncertainty, where the small solidity of land shelves through the warm, shell-strewn shallows of the beaches, or plummets from the cliffs of High Cove, into a vastness of water over which we have no control, and whose depths and behaviour we cannot predict. There is a pull both ways: further out into the wild intrigue of the sea, where the water is a delight against me, and back up the slope of the land to warmth and safety and the bonds of love. The land is changing, though; we will soon lose the safety of the island.

The sea is always unfixed, and tonight that is calming. It slops and clicks and chuckles against the rocks, while the land is silent, asleep. The sea is insomniac: it dozes, sometimes, on a still day, but with one eye open. It is companionable, now, alive and breathing. I wonder how soon I would be out of my depth, if I kept walking.

A light darts out again from the land behind me, and I realise that Patrick has gone down to the beach to look for me. I know how much even that short walk will make his legs hurt. If he doesn't find me there, he will probably call the coastguard, which would be awkward, but more importantly he will continue to walk, searching, and I am not there to stop him.

I turn round, and heave myself in my waterlogged boots back on to the jetty, and I walk back to the house. I meet Patrick on the path, and he says very little: he puts me to bed in some of his long thermal underwear with two hot-water bottles, and Skipp lies down on top of me until I sleep, with the sea around us murmuring and coughing through the night.

A week later, our belongings already packed off, Patrick and I step off the jetty on to Ernie's boat, and the island ghosts glance up for a second: Babs in her greenhouse, Gus on his quad bike, and Patrick, the fittest he'll ever be, waiting for a boat up to his thighs in the sea.

We look back towards the house, and then Patrick holds out his arms to me and smiles. I take his hand, and together we turn our faces to the shore.

Epilogue

Bee the cat is 17 now, her sister Ant already lost to arthritis and, in the way of the old, her world has shrunk. She ignores most of the rooms in our Devon house, and will inhabit only our bedroom, all amenities within easy reach. When we take her back to the island for a stay, I try to replicate this, but on the second day she seems suddenly to wake up. She requests her meals in the kitchen, where she always used to have them; she sleeps on the window seat, on various beds, in the middle of the dining room table; she insists on going outside for evening constitutionals.

Our early visits to the island after moving away are painful: we grieve for the land of lost content. The pink house has great compensations, not least eight newly fenced acres of ancient meadowland, hedged with holly and hawthorn, blackthorn and gorse, and by now home to several horses. It also has a chocolate-box charm, its asbestos roof replaced with thatch; enormous stone fireplaces with cloam ovens and shingled floors revealed under twentieth-century cover-ups; hand-carved beams fixed with ancient wooden pegs. We also have good neighbours and a local pub. But 'it's not the island', we can't help but remember, and it is a long time before we resolve to go there, alone, for longer than a few days, long enough to take the elderly cat. ('I *could* look after her,' my mother says, 'but she doesn't really like people, and she might die.') We have visited with my family, and with some of the good neighbours, but only when prompted by them. But on this trip, something shifts.

With Bee apparently ten years younger, and Skipp frolicking in a sea he'd once have said was much too cold, I feel the same change of energy, like a change in light. Our relationship with the house has become muddled, confusing; we have struggled to work out how best to look after it. But suddenly the sequence of tasks to perform in order to care for it is clear, and I clean and paint and organise as I did when we first came, and the house brightens. 'We're so lucky,' Patrick says, in front of the fire with the sea and the wind beside us.

Later, our Devon friends visit, with their two children. As I walk them up the beach from the boat, I can't resist telling Blue that he is exactly the same age as I was when I first came: seven and a half. 'Were you actually?' he asks, kindly. He is in sympathy with us and the island, and when he sees Jon and some volunteers start to take down the Chalet, he is upset. 'You used to stay in there!' he mourns. But it is nearly twenty years since it's been habitable, although Jon has patched it year on year with slices of island tree: the floor is shot, the roof is unwell, the whole structure is insecure.

I think of the brilliance of sunlight through its back window, the diamond sea, the astonishing deer who'd swum to us. I think of the candlelit evenings, the tea and whisky, the love. But as Blue says, almost tearful, 'It's so sad!' I can tell him without pretence that it's OK, that there will be a new and stronger building: that change is not something we need to be frightened of.

I could have told my seven-year-old self the same. That there are constants, in the vicissitudes of life, and that the island which I have just stepped on to will be one of the greatest. It embraced us, that first summer, in the clean air outside the bright rooms of Jetty Cottage; in the water which was a delight against us, swimming from Gull Island, Dunker Point, Jolly Roger Cove; in the novelty of life without a fridge, running water, electric light at night. It was the time of wholeness: life was circumscribed, complete, and perfect.

Forty years on, the island is no longer Babs and Attie, Lucky the dog and Tilly the cat; my mother making up our beds and cooking, ritually, soup and eggs on the first night of our holiday: but all of those things are part of it. So is our wedding, the loving restoration of the house, the good life of ducks and pigs, vegetables and bees, Gus and Sheila soothing in Smugglers and Ernie spinning yarns on *Pania*; so is my adolescence and young adulthood with the Proffitt-Whites, Katie and Ingela and Kath. Most of all, it is nearly a lifetime with my mother and my brothers, who still come there to stay with us now. They have undergone their own changes: but change has no bearing on the knowledge that stepping on to the island, or into the company of my family – those first island companions – is always to come home.

Perhaps Blue will have the same sense, one day, of the completeness of an island holiday: absorbed in the life of rock pools, thrilled by searching for secret tunnels, safe and loved in his family. Perhaps he will feel the same speechless joy as I still feel every time the boat crosses over the harbour bar and the island appears from nowhere: a turtle, a whale; a dark hump in the lucid sea, both astonishing and inevitable.

Although altered daily by the tides, the weather, the lives of its guardians, the island is always profoundly the same: stepping on to it is almost unbearably familiar. It remembers us, and some of its ghosts are ours, but most importantly it is uncompromisingly itself: forgiving and pitiless, indifferent and beguiling. It speaks to us with the voice of a gull, a seal, a storm, with the voices of the drowned and the departed, and the sound of it is dazzling.

The darkness of rock and tree shifts, unfurls, whenever you cross the water towards it: the white houses glow with little fires; the shingle beaches are silver in sunlight; the sea to the south brilliant in moon shafts.

Magical.

Acknowledgements

I drew extensively on the knowledge of experts on the local area and its history, and on a range of written sources, when writing the historical section of this book in particular. Mike Dunn's *The Looe Island Story* was invaluable as a comprehensive guide to the island's history, and the Time Team's excavations of Lammana priory, and the subsequent write-up by Wessex Archaeology, were also illuminating. Eric Berry's survey and report on Island House revealed unexpected secrets of the house itself.

Local historian John Southern, whose writings on the twentieth-century history of Looe are astonishingly prolific and detailed, provided wonderful insight into some previous owners of the island, as did Gavin Kingerlee and Dennis Malsher. Barbara Birchwood-Harper of the Guildhall Museum in Looe was particularly good on the smuggling history, and the late Sir John Trelawny's book *Islanders* gave a fascinating and completely plausible account of the eighteenth century smuggler inhabitants of the place.

Recent history from the mid sixties onwards was provided by Tony Pengelly, by Gus and Sheila Ravine, by Babs's reminiscences, and most of all of course by Attie's books *We Bought an Island* and *Tales from our Cornish Island*. Without Babs and Attie and their willingness to share their home, our lives and those of thousands of other holidaymakers, 'helpers' and friends would have been immeasurably poorer.

I am very grateful to the Arvon foundation who provided a grant for a week-long course, tutored by Horatio Clare and Miranda France, during which this book started to take shape. I am indebted to Miranda for her subsequent input, editing and encouragement, and to my agent Rowan Lawton for hers.

My mother, Chris Considine, not only introduced me to the island but also provided the epigraphs for the chapter headings. To her, and the many other friends and family who have been part of the island adventure: thank you most of all.